STOCK TRADING STRATEGIES FOR BEGINNERS

THE BIBLE FOR CREATING PASSIVE INCOME. HOW TO TRADE ONLINE WITH PROVEN MARKET STRATEGIES, TACTICS AND SECRETS TO START INVESTING IN THE MARKET FOR A LIVING

Henry Anderson

Stock Trading Strategies for Beginners

© Copyright 2020 by Henry Anderson.

All rights reserved.

This document is geared towards providing exact and reliable information with regards to the topic and issue covered. The publication is sold with the idea that the publisher is not required to render accounting, officially permitted, or otherwise, qualified services. If advice is necessary, legal or professional, a practiced individual in the profession should be ordered.

- From a Declaration of Principles which was accepted and approved equally by a Committee of the American Bar Association and a Committee of Publishers and Associations.

In no way is it legal to reproduce, duplicate, or transmit any part of this document in either electronic means or in printed format. Recording of this publication is strictly prohibited and any storage of this document is not allowed unless with written permission from the publisher. All rights reserved.

The information provided herein is stated to be truthful and consistent, in that any liability, in terms of inattention or otherwise, by any usage or abuse of any policies, processes, or directions contained within is the solitary and utter responsibility of the recipient reader. Under no circumstances will any legal responsibility or blame be held against the publisher for any reparation, damages, or monetary loss due to the information herein, either directly or indirectly.

Respective authors own all copyrights not held by the publisher. The information herein is offered for informational purposes solely, and is universal as so. The presentation of the information is without contract or any type of guarantee assurance.

The trademarks that are used are without any consent, and the publication of the trademark is without permission or backing by the trademark owner. All trademarks and brands within this book are for clarifying purposes only and are the owned by the owners themselves, not affiliated with this document.

TABLE OF CONTENTS

INTRODUCTION 5

CHAPTER 1 THINGS TO CONSIDER BEFORE INVESTING IN A STOCK 8

CHAPTER 2 HOW TO MAKE MONEY IN THE STOCK MARKET 13

CHAPTER 3 SELLING TIME IS IMPORTANT 16

CHAPTER 4 TOOLS OF THE TRADE 27

CHAPTER 5 TECHNICAL INDICATORS 34

CHAPTER 6 POSITION TRADING TACTICS AND STRATEGIES 37

CHAPTER 7 TRADING FOREX 45

CHAPTER 8 HOW TO FIND UNDERVALUED STOCKS 54

CHAPTER 9 THE FOREX CANDLESTICK 60

CHAPTER 10 STOCKS WHICH NEED A GROWING ECONOMY TO MAKE MONEY 66

CHAPTER 11 *DIVERSIFICATION* 69

CHAPTER 12 MONEY MANAGEMENT 73

CHAPTER 13 MINDSET AND PSYCHOLOGY 79

CHAPTER 14 RISK MANAGEMENT 88

CHAPTER 15 TIPS AND TRICKS 105

CHAPTER 16 WHAT IS THE STOCK MARKET? 116

CHAPTER 17 TERMS THAT IT IS IMPORTANT TO KNOW 122

CHAPTER 18 MASTER THE MYSTIC ARTS 128

CHAPTER 19 TOOLS FOR PROFITABLE TRADING **154**

CHAPTER 20 WHEN IS IT TIME TO SELL FOR A PROFIT? **167**

CHAPTER 21 VALUE INVESTING **172**

CHAPTER 22 HOW TO SAVE HUGE ON BLUE CHIP STOCKS **179**

CHAPTER 23 WHY YOU SHOULD CONSIDER SHORT SELLING STOCKS **181**

CHAPTER 24 STOCKS THAT TRADITIONALLY DO WELL DURING MARKET DOWNTURNS. **184**

CHAPTER 25 IDENTIFYING AND PICKING THE RIGHT GROWTH STOCKS **188**

CHAPTER 26 THE BASICS OF FUNDAMENTAL INVESTING **202**

CHAPTER 27 STOCK SCANNING AND BUILDING A WATCH LIST **218**

CHAPTER 28 10 COMMON MISTAKES BEGINNER INVESTORS MAKE AND HOW TO AVOID THEM **221**

CONCLUSION **226**

Introduction

Without an investment strategy that works, it is virtually impossible to earn more than we spend. For this reason, it is critical that we allocate a portion of our savings to make more money for us. Historically, stocks provide the highest potential returns over other asset classes, including bonds, savings accounts and real estate. It isn't unreasonable to expect long-term stock investment to range between 8-10% annually, depending on the time frame calculated. See appendix III for a long-term up-trending chart of the S&P 500, a widely used benchmark to evaluate how the overall stock market is performing. I will use the more conservative 8% figure as we move forward in this book.

This way, based on historical statistics, we have a minimum figure that should reasonably be achievable. It should be emphasized that investing in stocks is not without its risks. Short-term volatility (the amount of uncertainty or risk regarding price changes in a stock, mutual fund etc.) is one of the most notable of these risks. However, short-term volatility and other risks can be minimized by following a well-planned, intelligent long-term approach to stock investing, which is specifically what our wealth-building plan is all about!

How Much Money Do I Need to Start?

You do not need to be earning a large income to start utilizing our wealth-building plan. It is understood that, as a student, you will have a much lower income during your initial investment years than you will in your later years, so please do not worry. For a family with two income earners, each member will need to average slightly less than $700 per week in gross wages to adhere to the plan.

Investing in the stock market can be an extremely rewarding exercise if you invest the time to understand its nuances and how to leverage your knowledge and your stocks to make the most of it. Finding a mentor or joining local meetups in your city or where you live is a great way to discuss trading and bouncing ideas around with other like-minded people who share a passion for the stock market. While there is a lot that you can learn from books, courses, or online resources, there is a lot you can learn from face-to-face conversations and robust discussions on how to improve your trading strategy.

General operation of the stock market

Stocks could therefore be defined as a market in which buyers and sellers meet. But, unlike the traditional market, it is not the sellers who decide the price of their securities but the buyers. It is then the order book that accounts for the prices decided in this way. Ultimately, the more the securities of a stock market are required by the buyers, the higher the price goes up. On the contrary, when demand is weaker, their price falls.

The stock market on which securities can be traded is also called the "primary market". It is therefore on this market that companies can issue what are called "shares", that are then bought by investors, private individuals or professionals. Thanks to these purchases of securities, companies can obtain the money necessary to make investments. But the shares are not the only assets traded on this market since there can also be bonds or financial securities.

Investors' interest is speculative given that they buy a security at a price considered lower than the price that could subsequently reach for a gain or receive what are called "dividends" according to the economic performance of the issuing company of these securities becoming " shareholders ".

A market with international reach

Thanks to this system of securities and the advent of new technologies, the stock market has strongly developed on an international scale. Today there are almost as many stock exchanges as there are capitalist countries, although in most cases this market is virtual and does not include physical "trading rooms", the latter replaced by complex computer networks.

To better understand the importance of the stock exchange, know that in the single financial center of Milan, billions of euros are exchanged every day.

Chapter 1 Things to consider before investing in a stock

It is not true that to invest in stocks you have to have a lot of money. It is true that with equal choices a successful investment makes it proportionate to the money invested. But the opposite is also true, namely that if you make a mistake with so much money you lose more than if you make mistakes with a few. But the really important thing is that, with whatever sum you start, the stock exchange can give you earning opportunities. It all depends on how you invest. It is not an easy thing, as long as it is said, and it takes time and attention. There are two ways to earn from the stock market: cash out the dividends distributed periodically by the shares you have invested in; sell your shares at a higher price than the one you bought them. In short, in order to invest in shares and get a profit, one must know how to choose. Here are 7 things to keep in mind.

1. Plan the investment

The first advice that we can give you about financial investments, is about the planning of investments, or understand what are the best actions to buy and diversify your portfolio.

Even if you have never experienced this chain of events first hand, it isn't a problem. Sooner or later you have to learn.

In order to better diversify your stock portfolio and understand where to invest, we recommend opening a demo account.

The demo account allows you not only to plan investments, but also to:

- Carefully analyse the stock market on which you want to invest;
- Plan your investment strategies;
- Familiarize yourself with the platform;
- Get familiar with the market.

If you decide to buy shares in an unconscious manner and then open a real account and invest without the right measure, then prepare to say goodbye to your immense capital.

Of course this is not the most appropriate and wise way to invest.

2. Draw the investment plan you just made

To quote W. Edwards Deming, world-renowned essayist and quality management consultant:

"If you can't describe the process of what you're doing, you do not know what you're doing."

As for everything that requires a certain discipline, it is important to outline its investment strategy: in this way it will be easier to articulate it. Once your strategy is written, look at it to make sure it meets your long-term investment goals.

Writing and outline your strategy will give you a firm base to start again in times of chaos and will make you avoid making important investment decisions dictated by emotionality.

It offers you a clear outline to review and change if with time and experience you will notice defects or if you change your investment goals.

If you are a professional investor, having a written strategy in black and white will help your clients better understand the investment process you are proposing.

3. Learn the difference between investing an speculating

Understanding the difference between an investor and a speculator is very important. You need to know how to "use" the difference if you want to make the most out of your investments.

Before buying stocks you have to evaluate:

- what do you want to get from the markets;
- what is your personal level of risk tolerance;
- if you are investing;
- if your goal is to speculate on the markets;
- the time you have available to spend on investments.

If you want to get the maximum profit in a tight time, then you must have a considerable minimum time to devote to the study of markets and financial instruments. So you must understand the difference between speculator and investor.

What does a speculator do?

The speculator is that trader who buys and sells shares in order to make a profit in the short term; in this case we are talking about very narrow trade times ranging from a few minutes to a few weeks.

We do not talk about years or months.

They only take advantage of the price difference between the value of the sale and purchase of the deal.

The speculator's characteristic is that it is not interested in dividends distributed by listed companies.

What does an investor do?

Contrary to the previous one, the investor also defined as a long term investor, invests his capital by providing liquidity to the company.

In this case the investor will buy shares. The goal of an investor? Keep the stocks in his wallet for a prolonged period of time and make them profit!

This allows him to benefit from the detachment of the dividend that is added to the possible appreciation of the title.

Very important in this case is to understand what kind of investor you are. Pay close attention to this step because it is essential to earn with investments in the stock market. Most of the investor's operating strategies are based on fundamental analysis that is very different from those of a short-term trader or speculator.

4. Understand the importance of timing (and the impossibility of getting it right)

Very important is to understand when is the right time to buy and sell shares.

In this case the timing is an indispensable part to identify the stocks to be bought.

If the correct price levels are not identified, there could very well be the risk of entering the market at a risky point.

This could be unfavorable and does not allow us to accurately quantify the transaction's risk-return ratio.

Chapter 2 How to Make Money In the Stock Market

While buying your first stock can be exciting, if you want to make money as a trader, you have to sell the stock. Here, the general rule of thumb is to buy low and sell high. While I mentioned above that buying at the right time increases the possibility of turning a profit, selling at the right time guarantees you that profit. If you sell at the wrong time, any advantages you had from buying at the right time are negated.

Selling your stocks can be a very emotionally charged affair. Even if you have already made a profit, deciding whether to take those profits or hold on to the stock in the hope that it will rise even higher can be a difficult call. If your position is already in loss, it can be equally difficult to decide whether to sell at that point and cut your losses or hold on to the stock in the hopes that it will reverse and allow you to recoup the money you have lost so far. Keep in mind, however, that holding on could potentially lead to even bigger losses. Below, let's take a look at how to sell your stocks.

Making money in stocks

The first step is to determine why you want to sell. As a trader, the top reason for selling should be that your stock has hit your target price. Before getting into a position, you should have determined the price at which you will sell the stock. Once your stocks hit your target sell price, you can sell, since you will already have made your targeted profits. Having a target price can prevent you from making emotionally charged decisions, such as holding onto a stock for too long, which can wipe out your profits (and potentially lead to loss) in case the prices reverse.

Another reason to sell is when you receive information showing that the company's fundamentals are showing signs of stress. If you notice this, any other negative signs might lead to a mass panic, which will, in turn, cause the share price to nosedive. In such cases, it is best to sell while you still have some profit.

Index funds or individual stocks?

While there are a variety of options that you can go with when you join the stock market, most beginners are going to choose between two types of investments they may work with a stock mutual fund or an exchange-traded fund, or they may work with individual stocks.

Index funds and ETFs track an index. For example, you can work with an S&P 500 fund that will replicate that index by buying the stock of the companies that are in that fund. When you decide to invest in one of these funds, you will own small parts of each company in the fund. You can also decide to have several of these funds to help you build up a strong and diversified portfolio to invest in.

The other option is to work with some individual stocks. If you want to invest in one specific company, you can choose to purchase a single share or several if you have the money. This is a good way to dip your toes into the water and see how it goes. Building a portfolio that is diversified with this option is possible, but it will take you more time because these are usually more expensive to purchase at the beginning.

The upside of going with the stock mutual funds is that they are set up to be diversified. This is a great way to reduce the amount of risk you will run when you join the stock market. But it is very unlikely that you will see a huge rise in prices as you can sometimes see with individual stocks.

The upside of choosing to go with individual stocks is that a wise pick can earn you a big profit, but the odds that one stock will be able to make you rich are very slim. The risks are higher with this kind of option as well.

For those who are just getting started with the stock market, it is often best to go with the mutual funds. This helps you build up your portfolio and reduce your risks as things start to grow. You can always go with an individual stock after you have some time to grow your money and can take on more risks.

Chapter 3 Selling Time is Important

Now that you know how to open an account at a brokerage firm and buy stocks in the open market and through spinoffs, it is time for you to know when to sell them. You need to build up a powerful defensive wall for your investments. The stock market is not about winning every time. At every corner you will find a shark ready to suck the blood out of your investment ventures. John twice washed his hands off his investments just because he was too naïve to perceive the dangers that came his way in this business. But this doesn't mean you shouldn't step in the game. It is natural you see. Just like roses bloom within the thorns, and every good thing has its perils, the stock investment business also has its risks. That's why you need to build a pre-determined defense to guard yourself against decisive losses. When it comes to stock investing, you can make countless mistakes pertaining to the selection of the stocks and the timing of purchases, as well as the timing of sales. A single poor decision can incur somewhat heavy losses to your investment. It can get pretty nasty at times. How well you fare in the stock market depends on how in-depth the information is that you have garnered about stock investing, how many quality books you have read, and how better and concrete your analysis is. But no matter how better you have prepared and how smart your attitude is, you will not be right every single time.

The key to saving your skin when the odds are against you is to cut down on your losses, briskly. Markets are affected by a complex pattern of factors, like the international, political, and economic situations, trade restrictions, imposition of tariffs, wars, and terrorism. They can nosedive like the infamous 1929 stock market crash. You should not be worried about their fall. Instead you need to be better prepared to know when the markets are going to nosedive, and take appropriate action that could save your investment. The secret to winning in the stock market is to cut your losses when you are on the wrong side of the situation. The key is to know when you have made a bad investment and then take decisive action quickly and pull out from the market. But how will you know when you are not right? If you have stock in an electronics company, and its price falls below your purchase price, that means you have made a bad decision, and that it is possible you will have to pay for that decision with your own money. So, are the people who become enormously successful in the stock market business always right or extremely lucky? Successful people are neither lucky nor are they right all the time. They are the ones who have made lots of mistakes. Luck is all about hard work and nothing else. Successful people are those that fail, but never stop trying until they succeed. Moreover, each big success takes time. So, coming back to the winning strategy! John says that he found from years of experience that only one or two out of every ten stocks works the way he wants and are capable of giving back huge returns. John always bought a set of stocks and then he watched very closely to identify those couple of stocks that would work for him. As for the other stocks that don't work well, consider them as bad choices and wait for the time they take off. It is going to take many potential failures before you it the jackpot. Microsoft sprinted from 100% to 1000% in 1986-1992. International Game Technology did the same in 1991-1993. They amazed investors. Sometimes you just have to be patient.

Thoughts of a Common Investor

John is a typical investor, probably much like you. He watches the market patterns and keeps records of the transactions in the market, like what he buys, at which price he buys, and what the current price is after he owns it. He keeps a red diary in his front pocket, just like Moriarty did in one of the Sherlock Holmes movies. He guards it with his life. Sometimes I wonder if he has loved anything more than his red diary. Whenever he is about to sell a stock, John goes through the records to see the price at which he bought it and compares it with the current price of the stock. In case of a higher current price, he sells the stock. Otherwise, he waits for the right moment to sell it for profit. John, in his earlier stage of investing, used to think that a stock that didn't give him the profit he was looking for should be done away with, never to be touched again in future. For example, if you bought a stock for $50 a year ago and its current price is $52, this doesn't mean it will keep a low price in the in future. But that's how common investors think when they enter the stock market. This thinking is superficial and narrow. With the passage of time this approach broadens. At least

I hope it does. A common investor considers it a loss when he or she sells a stock at a lower price than the price at which they had purchased the stock. What they don't understand is that they have already incurred heavy loss by being unable to sell when the price was higher. So, in the world of stocks this is considered a double loss. In simple words, if you hold a stock for two months and sell it at a loss, your loss is not just confined to the money you have lost in per share price, but it is bigger than that. You have blocked your own money in a useless stock for two months and failed to sell when it offered profits. For winning in the stock market understanding the nature of loss is very important.

Stock market is akin to any physical business. It demands your time and energy and focus to give you results. A friend of mine had a garments store in India. He had a huge diversity of clothes at the store. All the designs like Lehnga (a kind of skirt), Dhoti Shalwaar (a kind of trouser), and Choori daar (leggings) sold like hot cakes every time he brought new designs and colors. But there was one thing that he couldn't sale - the Patiala shalwar (a loose form of trousers). He was worried because his money was blocked in the stock of Patiala shalwar. One day a lady bought a couple, but later returned to buy the Choori Daar. Understanding the situation and need to get our from under the tied up money, he put the old dogs on sale for 20% off. After that, 40% off in order to get rid of them and recover his money. The day he did away with the last of them, he ordered the other three types of pants that were hot in demand. Well, that's how business moves on. You go with the demand. The key is to move on fast after taking a fall. Same is the case in the stock market. In case you made a wrong decision and are about to fall, sell the old dog, and save yourself a heavy loss. John has adopted a simple strategy for protection from losses. He analyzes the situation he invests in and makes an educated estimate of potential profits and losses. I have already written in detail on the subject of studying a stock's history. That's what you have to base your mathematics on. Fly with the rules. Know the inside of the game. Be the game. A suggestion here is that you should write down the price you have to sell in case you are suffering from a loss. Similarly, you have to write down the expected high price at which you want to make profits. Don't be greedy when the days are in your favor. Stay sensible and wait for the market to touch the price you had written down in your red diary. Once the stock hit the price level, don't wait for it to go higher. Sell it and bag the profit. Similarly, if it comes down, don't wait for it to reverse to the top. Sell it and save your investment. This is the simple strategy to be and stay a winner in the stock market.

Confine your Losses if you want to be a Winner

Common investors should make and adopt a firm plan to try to limit the loss on initial invested capital. In this sense, you need to limit your losses to 5% on average and to 7% maximum. This is a quick loss cutting plan that you need to follow in order to lower your chances of failure. In simple words, if you by a stock for $100, you should cut down the losses to $7 maximum. That's how you need to plan your losses. If you don't plan for it, you lose the game. The losses will one day get out of control. By confining your loss to 7% it means its below the buying price. If you have already made considerable profits and the price is now fluctuating as it does in the stock market, you can afford to take the 7% loss, and wait for the price to once again move higher.

It all depends on your particular situation. You can afford to lose a chunk of your profits only for the sake of recovering the loss in a short time in future, but you cannot afford to lose your capital. Once it falls down to bargain price, you should not hesitate to sell. Get out of the deal and start afresh. Losing your capital in the stock market is not the way to win.

Add Extra Insulation and Protection to Your Investments

When you cut down your losses, you are adding extra protection to your investments. It is like an insurance policy. You are saving vital capital for your future ventures. John said that there were lots of times when he sold a stock in fear of losing capital and the same day the stock reversed and started rising again. Yes, it will happen, sometimes often. You might think you made a wrong decision. You might get frustrated. John had the same feelings. He wanted to smash his head into the wall sometime! The rebound in the price of the sold stock just maddened him at times. If you couldn't make profit, you must realize that you can incurred heavy losses. You are saved. An insurance policy is meant to protect your home from fire in case an incident takes place. What if it doesn't? Will you say it was a bad decision to sign up for insurance? No! It wasn't a bad decision, which is apparent from the fact that you will buy the same insurance the next year. Same is the case of cutting down on your losses. It is like protection for you against serious losses to your capital. You can't tell the mood of the market. *Don't argue with the market:* John had a friend in Asia who had investments in the stock market. He bought shares in PAEL (an electronic manufacturing company) at $30 per share. The share price reduced to $20. He bought more of them in the hope that when the market rebounded, he would bag enormous profits, as he had settled his average share price by securing more at a lower rate. Share price fell to $15. About half the value of the price at which he bought. He lost half the capital. He argued with the market, and tried to outsmart it, but he was defeated. The rule should be not to argue with the market. Just go with the flow. Follow the rules I am telling you and be happy with your capital and the earnings in hand. People start get angry when the market doesn't behave as they expect it to be. Take care of your mental and physical health by abiding to the simple rules of the game. Small losses are not going to hurt you that much. You still have most of the capital that you can use to recover the losses and earn more profit. The only thing you should keep in mind is that no matter if all the stocks you have sold have gone up, you have succeeded in cutting down potential losses. You have achieved the critical objective of keeping your losses small. Just don't wait. You have all the money to try your luck once again in another stock. You can be a winner next time. Sitting and waiting for a stock to recover not only causes frustration, but also a loss of time and heavy cash. Still, some investors argue that it is a good idea to wait for the stock to rebound and bag profits. Yes, it can rebound and most of the time it will. But what if it can't? You will lose your hard-earned money in a single go, and you will have no money to invest in other stocks to recover your loss. *Don't risk it all:* A small wound can heal in a matter of days, but if you don't treat it then it can grow deeper and maybe even become infected and dangerous. Stocks are similar. Treat it at an early stage. Don't risk it all. Only risk it if you have loads of cash in your safe and that you can afford to lose. Your capital has to be protected. A friend once asked me what if a company is about to launch a new product in a couple of weeks? Well, naturally there is a chance that the stocks will perform really well, but still, are you willing to risk your capital for it? *Don't be an egoist; accept the defeat:* The biggest hurdle in cutting down your losses is to convince yourself that you were wrong. You may have made a bad choice. You have selected the wrong stock, or your timing of the investment was not right. But this is normal business in stock market. Every person is wrong at times in the stock market. That's how this business works. Just focus on controlling your losses and you will be on the road to winning. *Speculation goes on:* Speculation is part of the stock market business. It happens in all common stocks. It influences the losses and the profits. A stock that is under 50% loss started with 10% or 15%, but it is speculation that has pushed it beyond 50%. That's why it is recommended by John, and of course, me for you to pull out of the stocks at 7% loss below your purchase price, and put on a happy face. You might be thinking if the stock gets out of hand and reaches a 10% loss, should you wait? Never. Sell it at 10% or even 15%. Your sole objective should be to save the money you have in your hand. You can recover 10% loss easily, and even 15% loss after a considerable effort. How about recovering 50% loss? You will have to double the profits in your next transactions if you suffer from a 50% loss. Can you double it in a matter of week? How many stock brokers can double in a week? Just a few lucky dudes! Are you sure you will be among the lucky handful? Stocks can be pressed down due to speculation. Once speculators succeed in putting the stock on a selling streak, it is hard for it to recover short-term. A common investor can't be sure what is going on inside a company because its hidden it from the markets. So, you never know if a stock goes down, how many days, weeks, months and even years it will take to recover.*Are you thinking about a long-term investment?* Are you saying that you are a long-term investor and that's why you are safe from the lows? Well, you're probably wrong, my friend. If your stocks shed 25% in value, your annual yield will drop down considerably because of the fact that you are not making the profit you were supposed to make, or you will have made in another stock. Winning in the stock market is directly proportional to a disciplined approach towards buying and selling stocks. Make certain rules and strictly follow them. Either you can read this book and jot down the important points to care about, or you can sail into the stormy ocean, ride the waves, sink at times, and swim ashore, and learn a hard lesson in the end. But that's the path that's a bit hard to tread on. Even if you are a skilled surfer on stormy waves, you need to carry some basic knowledge and tips to get started.

The Big NO: When John started in the stock market, a broker, a naïve one, asked him to average down the price of a stock. John bought Red Plush Cosmetics' shares at $40 per share. The price stooped to $30 in two weeks. The broker advised him to buy more of the stock at a low price to improve his average buying price. The stock didn't recover for over a year. John suffered a big loss. What he did after recovering financially and emotionally was to fire the broker and hire a new one, and smart one. He actually asked the broker the same question in a pre-hiring chit chat, 'what would you advise if I buy a stock and its price drops?' The broker responded with a single word, 'SELL!' John didn't ask anything more. Hired! You are simply not going to start a love affair with a stock. Get in and get out. Don't stay to adjust your averages of a stock. That's a possible trap. Investors go for adjusting the averages to get out when the situation turns into their favor. There is no problem with this thinking, but you never know what is boiling up inside a company. You can't exactly predict the driving factors behind the price fluctuation of a particular stock. They might have had a non-selling product on the market. They might be laying off heavily due to some kind of heavy loss. In addition, as I already mentioned, the stock price may be dropping in the wake of some serious speculation.

Stock market moves, like any other market, on the principle of supply and demand. It means there is nothing wrong with your approach. Perhaps investors don't want to buy a particular stock anymore. Get rid of the Patiala Shalwaar and minimize the risk.

Staying Confident in the Stock Market is the Key to Success

Losses not only hurt your bank balance, but they also hurt your self-confidence. You disapprove of your methods, which hurt your brain, and that's not good for you. You are in need of a healthy self-esteem to be successful in the stock market. If you start becoming reluctant to invest or become fearful while making a decision, you'll struggle to make a good decision. And if you make any, it is going to be a bad one for sure. It all happens because you are bitten by losses that were supposed to be profits. That's the reason you need to cut down your losses in order to stay confident. Investors usually don't take the time to do their homework. They don't study the situation before entering it. In an effort to get out unharmed, they get stuck in more harm. The decision of when to get out of a stock market is more important than when to enter. You have saved your investment; you have insulated your confidence. And that's what you need the most in the long haul until you have enough experience that your brain automatically triggers the alarm whenever a situation develops that may lead you to a potential loss. Until then, watch out for the risks, keep your investment safe, and stay confident in order to be a winner.

Chapter 4 Tools of the Trade

Even when compared to other types of trading, the tools you use as a day trader are extremely important if you hope to generate a profit on a regular basis. Thanks to the tight timeframes that day traders typically operate under, every second can literally be the difference between success and failure which means the platforms, software and tools you use are ultimately just as important as the strategies you employ and the stocks you pick to trade. What follows is a list of things that every day trader should have on hand in order to ensure as much success as possible.

Tools

The right hardware: While you don't necessarily need the latest and greatest in computer hardware in order to run most types of trading software, that doesn't mean you can get by with the bare minimum either. The better your computer, the faster and smoother this software will run and the less lag and fewer crashes you will experience. First and foremost, it is important that you have adequate RAM which will make it easier to multitask without issue as you will frequently have several different programs as well as your web browser open at the same time. Additionally, as your software needs increase, the base level of hardware required will do the same.

While these costs can easily add up dramatically if you have to purchase an entire new rig all at once, there will rarely be a need to do so. Rather, you can purchase parts overtime as needed, or when they are on sale, in a more piecemeal fashion most of the time. With this strategy, you can grow your hardware capabilities slowly as your need for the increased power manifests itself.

As you get more serious about day trading, you are also likely going to want to run at least 2 monitors at a time, if not more, which will allow you to dedicate one to trading and the other to research and tracking results. This will mean you will likely need a better video card with enough HDMI ports to account for the additional monitor inputs. Once this is done, depending on the quality of your system, and its available cooling power, you may need to look into liquid cooling solutions as well to ensure that things don't overheat in the midst of an important trade.

Regardless, you are going to want to invest in the best internet speed available that your current system can reasonably take advantage of. The current high-end standard is 1 gigabyte MBPS which can be found in most major markets, though something around 100 MBPS is typically fast enough for most systems. In addition to having access to the speed, you are going to need to be sure that your router and modem can keep up as well or they will bottleneck your efficiency to a noticeable degree. When you contact your internet service provider, you will also want to consider reinstalling a landline as a type of emergency backup in case you find yourself unable to make a specific trade in any other fashion. While this might seem like overkill, the $10 per month will seem reasonable the first time you find yourself using it to place a major trade and you can think of it as a hardline to your broker in case the worst occurs.

Brokerage: Many traders stick with the first brokerage they come across without ever thinking twice about it. This can be a serious mistake, however, as an experienced trader has needs that are frequently quite different than those of a beginner. As such, once you get used to the day trading experience it will generally behoove you to reevaluate your choice of broker and determine if you ultimately made the right decision. First thing in order to determine the best options for what you are looking for, the best place to start is on your favorite day trading website and see what the people who frequent their forums have to say. After you have determined a suitable list, the next thing you will want to do is determine the fees that they charge in exchange for the services that they offer. If you have already determined what trading platform or online tools that you prefer then it is important to make sure that the brokerages you are looking at support them as not all brokerages support all trading platforms. Otherwise you risk having to learn an entire new platform from scratch.

Additionally, it is very important that you choose a brokerage that is based in your home country or at least in a country that provides proper oversight when it comes to day trading. While many foreign brokerages might offer cheaper fees, putting your money into the hands of a company without direct oversight means that if that company suddenly disappears, your trading capital will go with it.

Finally, it is important to make a concentrated effort when it comes to determining the type of customer service the brokerages you are interested in provide. In order to determine this, you will want to do more than listen to reviews which can easily be skewed in one way or another, it is instead best to see for yourself. This means you are going to want to call the brokerage personally and see how long it takes for you to speak with a real person. While you won't have to actually call your brokerage very often, when you do it is likely to be an emergency which means you are going to want the time it takes to find someone to talk to, to be as short as it possibly can be.

As a new customer, it is likely that you will receive a call back from someone associated with the brokerage who will try and sell you their service. If this call takes more than one business to occur then you will know that you are better off going somewhere else. After all, if the company treats new customers with that level of disdain, consider how much worse things will be once they already have your money and aren't actively trying to make a good impression. Finally, assuming that their customer service is up to snuff, you will also want to email them with questions a few different times, just to see what their level of response is like. While this process may be a bit time consuming, once you find a brokerage that is on point, it will be more than worth the effort in the long run.

Online trading tools: There are plenty of different tools online that claim to help you maximize your trade efficiency so the ones you choose to use are ultimately up to you. First things first, you are going to want to find a financial calendar that works for you to ensure that you don't miss any important dates when it comes to financial earnings reports. The program you choose should automatically populate with various important events as well as offer many different customizable dates and provide details on multiple different markets.

If you ever trade in the forex market then you will want to find a good currency convertor that shows any changes to specified currencies in real time. You will also want a currency convertor that shows the range a specific currency pair has operated in over a predetermined period of time.

Additionally, you will want to ensure that you have a calculator that makes it easy to determine pivot points along with Fibonacci numbers. These tools will make it easy for you to keep up to date on relevant trends and help you stay informed on relevant indicators that it is otherwise easy to miss if you aren't careful. Along similar lines, you are going to want to track down a heat map that is reliable and that shows you the trades that are currently trending along with a volatility monitor to make it easy for you to keep tabs on the mood of the market.

Popular Platforms

There are so many popular platforms online these days that finding the right one can be something of a chore. The list collected here will simplify this search somewhat as it lists those that are currently at the top of the list. This doesn't mean that you shouldn't do your own research if you have a lot of specific requirements, it is only here to point you in the right direction.

OptionsHouse.com: This is a trading platform that just offers the basics which is perfect for those who just want to focus on trading. It offers a variety of easily modifiable tools, zero minimum account balance and a flat commission rate of $4.95 per trade.

InteractiveBrokers.com: For those who like all the frills possible, this site offers a wide range of perks including classes for new traders and a variety of trading aids. They do require a minimum trade balance of $10,000, however, though those under 25 aren't held up to this level of scrutiny. They take $.005 of each traded share and include trading options for precious metals, forex, futures and more.

Ameritrade.com: This platform is considered one of the best on the market today and charges a flat rate fee of $9.99 for each trade. They feature a low required balance, several trading platforms based on what the client is looking for and access to especially curated research. They also offer an additional trading platform known as Trade Architect which is designed for those looking for something straightforward and simple.

Tradestation.com: This platform's main claim to fame is its extremely fast order execution rate and charges anywhere from $5 to $10 depending on the volume of the trade. Their required minimum balance is $5,000 and a $99 monthly subscription fee which is waved if you hit a large enough trade volume each month. Their trade platform is also lauded for its robust feature set.

Chapter 5 Technical Indicators

A technical indicator is a pattern you see in price levels, which are designed to help you predict the future price. There are various indicators, such as candlestick patterns, relative strength index, MACD, money flow index, Stochastics, and Bollinger bands. Sounds complicated, right?

There are definitely some technical indicators that are more difficult to learn. We will not focus on those in the beginner's guide. The only technical indicator that will be explained is the support and resistance pattern.

Support and Resistance

Pull up a price chart for a stock. Any stock. Look at the graph. Do you see a low price the stock seems to hit often? For example, if the price is $5 per share to $6 per share, but the price never falls below $5, you have a support line. The stock is constantly returning, over a period of three months, to around $5, but never below $5.

Now look at how high the stock has increased from the $5 mark. Let's say the price has gone up to $15 once, but over the same three-month period, the stock was mostly around $13 per share, before it would return to $5.

In March, the stock went from $5 to $13 back to $5 four times. For April, the stock did the same thing, but it did these 5 times. Now it is May. The news indicates the stock will continue to have interest, but there will be nothing to push it beyond the 60-day high of $15 per share.

The support is $5 and the resistance is $13. If you set up a trade where you buy in the next time it hits $5.10, you will stay in the stock until it has an automatic order to sell at $12.90. You have earned a profit because you bought in at $5.10 and sold it at $12.90. The profit is 12.90-5.10=7.80. It means for the shares you purchased, you made $7.80. If you bought 100 shares, your profit would be $780 for the entire trade, less any commission fees. If you did this 5 times in one month, your profit would be $3,900.

Of course, this is an example. A stock could break the support and go lower than $5 and it could break the resistance, where it goes over $13, rises to $20, and then falls to $13, where it sets a new support at $12.50 and a new resistance of $21.

This is why studying the graphed price levels, looked at the 52- week high, the current high for a selected period, and the high and low for the day, will help you see what the current and long term support and resistance patterns are.

You will choose a period of time-based on how you want to trade. If you are leaving your money in the stock for two months, you need to know the 52-week high and low. You also need to see the price movements for the previous two months to analyze if there has been a bigger pattern, such as a steady increase or steady decline in the price volume over time. For day traders, they are only concerned about the 24-hour period, and whether the overall pattern is a steady increase or decrease.

Trading Steps

1. Find a stock.
2. Assess the news, economic reports, projected growth, and company share movements.
3. Determine if there is talk of a projected price point or a break in the support or resistance positions.
4. Study the 52-week high, current high and lows, and the high and lows for the past few months, weeks, or days based on your trade position.
5. Your research might determine if this will be a long term, short term, or day trade.
6. Create an entry point based on the low price.
7. If the trade is fulfilled, put an order on it to protect your profit.
8. The trade order, such as stop loss, limit, or trailing stop will determine if the order is closed.
9. Set your entry and exit points based on the support and resistance patterns.

Chapter 6 Position Trading Tactics and Strategies

In this chapter, we will look at how you can implement some wise position trading strategies in order to help you reduce your level of risk and boost your understanding of how you can make the most of your investment decisions.

One word of caution: if you choose to engage in position trading, I will encourage you to do your homework on the investment vehicle you are purchasing. In addition, it pays to be on top of every development with regard to your open positions.

Don't be afraid to pull the trigger on a deal if you don't feel comfortable with the way your position is trending. As such, you may have to liquidate your position sooner than you anticipated if you don't feel confident about the likelihood of your security rebounding.

That being said, let's discuss some of the ways you can engage in position trading.

Commodities

Commodities are a good place to start with position trading.

Often, commodities will have sharp fluctuations in the short term but may be poised for long-term gains.

Let's consider oil as an example.

Oil is a highly volatile commodity which depends on a host of factors in order to determine its price. The factors that come into play when setting oil prices boil down to supply and demand. As long as the supply is up, the price will be down. And as long as supply is down, the price will go up.

Oil is dependent on supply as demand will virtually remain the same. If anything, demand will go up when oil is cheaper, and it will level off as it gets more expensive.

Now, when you invest in oil, there are two main ways in which you can do this:

One, through a futures contract.

And two, through an ETF.

When you purchase futures contracts on oil, you are basically purchasing oil production three months in advance. If you are not actually an oil refiner, you really won't have any need to take physical delivery of the oil.

So, when you purchase a futures contract, you can then sell the contract for a premium on the price you paid. This will entitle you to a profit as a seller while the buyer may benefit from paying a lower price on oil.

The other type of way you can invest in oil is through an ETF.

An oil ETF is a pool of money grouped together and invested in oil. Generally speaking, the funds raised through oil ETFs will be most likely invested in oil futures. Since investors in oil ETFs want exposure to the commodity but are unconcerned about taking physical delivery of the commodity, you can earn interest on your investment in the ETF.

This is a great way for you to earn some passive income while having the option of selling your stake in the ETF and making some cash on the sale of your position.

Investing in commodities may end up providing you with a great opportunity to play off a longer-term trend in which prices are rising.

What about Forex?

Forex is another great opportunity for you to engage in position trading.

Since Forex pits currency combinations against one another, fluctuations are certain to be plentiful.

As such, short-term fluctuations in Forex markets can wreak havoc on the sanity of day traders.

For position traders, the longer-term approach may favor them particularly during times of economic downturn among countries.

For example, if you pair up the US Dollar versus the Euro, the trends observed in both the Dollar and the Euro may determine whether one currency will gain in value relative to the other.

This implies that if Europe enters some sort of economic downturn which puts pressure on their currency, you might consider betting against the Euro.

On the other hand, if the US Dollar Index is declining due to strong economies throughout the world, you might choose to bet against the Dollar and stock up on Euros.

Either way, short-term profits might be non-existent since the market fluctuations affect pennies on the dollar, at best. But if you consider a longer-term approach, you will be able to make much larger profits since swings in currency can take longer than anticipated.

Consequently, Forex traders can take advantage of the shift in the economic landscape of individual countries which end up reflected in their currency's valuation.

Bonds

Bonds are often overlooked when considering position trading.

Bonds provide excellent opportunities to allocate funds into safer investment vehicles which are also highly liquid. This means that investors can quickly liquidate their bonds and get cash whenever they need to.

Most importantly, bonds come in all shapes and sizes. For example, there are 3 and 6-month bonds and range all the way up to 30 years.

The shorter-term bonds provide excellent opportunities for investors to put some money into solid investments without tying up their money for too long.

As such, traders can hold their positions for longer periods of time while collecting interest payouts from bonds.

Long-term bonds such as 10-year ones may offer better returns in the long run but would be better suited for passive investors who wish to lock up their investments with very specific, long-term goals in mind such as retirement and paying for college education.

Precious Metals

Precious metals (gold, silver, platinum, and palladium) don't get a lot of love from day traders.

These metals are usually traded as commodities and can be traded either through futures or ETFs.

Investors who wish to gain exposure to precious metals may do so by buying into an ETF and riding out the long-term waves that come with these commodities.

In general, investors tend to seek out precious metals when currencies such as the Dollar take a downturn or if other commodities such as oil, show considerable fluctuations.

As such, investors may look toward precious metals as a means of riding out longer periods of volatility. Nevertheless, day traders tend to shy away from precious metals and industrial metals, such as copper and aluminum since they offer very little regarding gains in the short term.

For an investor to make considerable gains from investing in metals, they would need to hold onto their positions for extended periods of months, at least several months, or even years, before they could see the true benefit of investing in this type of asset class.

Index Funds

Index funds are funds which don't invest in individual stocks, but rather invest in a collective approach following a major stock index. For instance, an index fund pegged to the Dow Jones would contain a stock of several companies traded on the Dow.

This would ensure exposure to several individual stocks while providing a greater degree of diversification in the types of stocks themselves.

As such, traders may choose to hold on to these funds for months at a time, especially when the markets are bullish.

Index funds provide decent returns and reduce risk considerably as fluctuations in individual stocks can be offset by the fluctuations in others. Therefore, if one stock falls, and others rise, this offsetting function will allow the investor to gain by the market's overall trend.

Index funds are also highly liquid, especially in times of consistent market gains. When markets are booming, index funds gain quite a bit of popularity from average investors and day traders alike.

Investing in index funds may also be a part of a more conservative investment approach since investors and traders will only lose money if the markets, as a whole, tank in unison. This can happen in times of economic shocks and devastating events, such as 9/11. Barring anything like 9/11, markets remain relatively steady, and investors can generally decipher the overall market trends.

Final Thoughts on Position Trading

I would encourage you to take a closer look at position trading especially if you are looking for a less trade-intensive approach. Since fees and commissions can add up, you can look to the types of investments which won't require you to engage in high-frequency trading.

Also, there is an important benefit that can be derived from position trading: passive income.

If you play your cards right, you can generate a decent amount of passive income just by making a series of trades at specific points in time. Since you won't be required to be at your desk at all times, you can hang back somewhat and let your investments do the work for you.

One word of caution though: when you are a position trader, you cannot take your eyes off the ball. If you do, you might miss changes in economic and market conditions which may adversely affect your portfolio. When that happens, you might sustain losses before you are able to react accordingly.

So, even if you are not keen on making a large number of trades, you still need to make sure you don't miss what's going on in financial markets.

Chapter 7 Trading Forex

Trading Forex can be a very interesting hobby for other people in the current world. This form of a thrilling kind of hobby can be a great source of generating revenue. To lighten up people's light, over five trillion US dollars are traded in a day. To formally understand the trade, the process is divided into three namely learning basics terminologies in Forex, opening of an online Forex brokerage account and starting the trade.

Learning Basic Terminologies in Forex

1. Understanding basic Forex terminology

The first two terminologies an individual is supposed to understand are the base currency and quote currency. During the Forex trade, two currencies are always traded. The currency that is being got rid is referred to as the base currency. The other currency being bought is known as the quote currency. For a person to buy the quote currency, he or she will be guided by the foreign exchange rates. The foreign exchange rates help a person to know how much he or she will have to spend.

There are two positions in the process of trading currencies. A person can choose to take a long term or short-term position. A long-term position involves a person buying the base currency and in turn selling the quote currency. On the other hand, buying the base currency and selling the base currency is referred to a trader taking a short-term position. The trader always has a price which he or she can willingly buy the base currency in exchange to get quote currency. This price is always known as a bid fee.

Bid prices can change during the process of broking currencies. This leads to the rise of an asking price. It is the price an individual is able to sell the base currency in return to gain the quote currency. Bid price mostly is the best price available in the market a person can buy the other currency. The difference between the asked price and the bid price is known as a spread.

2. Reading the Forex quote

There are two numbers an individual will observe in the Forex quote. The numbers present include the bid price and the asking price. The bid price is always situated on the left side while the asking price is always situated on the right side.

3. Descending on what currency a person wants to buy and sell

This process starts with a person predicting an economy. An individual can take a common economy like the United States of America economy. An individual can believe of the US economy declining. This situation is bad for the American dollar since it will depreciate in terms of value. Therefore, the situation will lead to a person offloading the dollar in exchange for the other forms of currency which strong economies.

The individual can look at a country trading position to know which currency to buy and sell. The better country to look at is that with a high amount of goods that are inconsistent demand. There are high possibilities for such a country to have high numbers of exports and thus make more money from international and local trade. The phenomenon will be a strong boost to a country and in turn, boosting the currency. The information favoring such a country gives a trader the best currency to invest in.

The decision over which currency to buy and sell can be determined by the political temperatures of a country. The most crucial times are during the elections in a country. The currency is approximated to rise if a person winning the election has an agenda aligning to favorable fiscal policies. The currency can be favorable to buy if the regulations on economic growth are loosened. The action likely leads to an increase in the value of a country's currency.

Economic reports of a country can also help a person in making the decision on which currency to buy and sell. An individual can choose to focus on a country's Gross Domestic Income or a country's Per Capita Income. Other information that can be critical includes the employment rate and inflation rate. This critical information will provide a trader with accurate information about the value of the currency to buy and sell.

4. Learning how to calculate profits

The process involves a person's ability to be able to measure the value change in two currencies. Pip measures the difference between the two traded currencies. One pip is usually equated to 0.0001change in value. A good example can be drawn from an exchange of the Euro to the American dollar. If the trade of EUR/USD shifts from 2.646 to 2.647, the value of the currency is said to have increased by ten pips. The next step involves an individual multiply the pips numbers his or her account with the current exchange rates. The value got will help an individual know if he has made a gain or a decrease in his account.

Opening of Online Forex Brokerage Account

1. Researching of different brokerages

There are several factors an individual is supposed to consider while choosing his brokerage. These factors to consider include:

- Going out for the experience. This should be the main consideration when choosing a brokerage individual or a company. The person or company is decided on is supposed to have a minimum experience of ten years in the market. The experience will be able to help a person to know the company is on track. Experience also indicates the company or an individual is good at taking care of his or her clients.
- One is supposed to ensure that the brokerage is regulated. The regulation of brokerages is mostly done by the chief oversight body. It is very

pleasing if a broker chose on has a total submission to the government. The situation gives an individual reassurance on broker transparency and honesty. There are several oversight bodies across the globe and they include;

    a. United Kingdom; Financial Conduct Authority
    b. Switzerland; Swiss Federal Banking Institution.
    c. Australia; Australian Securities and Investment Commission.

- The types of available products by the broker are also another factor for an individual to consider. There are some factors that help an individual to know if the brokerage has a wide business reach and a large client base. One of the determining factors these occurrence is also trading securities and commodities.
- A person interested in the forex market is supposed to be a careful reader of reviews. It is because some dishonest brokers can write reviews that are false to build a good brand for themselves. These reviews written help an individual to get the flavor of the broker. However, an individual is supposed to take these brokers with a granule of the brackish.
- Visiting the website of a broker is not supposed to be left out. This website is supposed to have a good professional look. The links provided on the website are supposed to be functional also. If there are any doubts on the website, an

individual is supposed to steer clear from the broker.
- Checking on the transactional cost of each trade is also advantageous to a person interested to be successful in Forex trade. An individual is supposed to check how much the bank will charge him or her to wire funds into his or her Forex account.
- An individual is supposed to be able to focus on the essentials. These essentials include focusing on good clientele support and transactions that are easy and transparent. An individual is supposed to be attracted to a broker who has a good reputation.

2. Requesting information about opening an account

There are two forms of account an individual can open to be able to trade in the Forex market. An individual chose to open a personal account or he or she can choose to open a managed account. Having a personal account will help an individual to manage his or her account. On the other hand, having a managed account tasks the broker with the ability to execute the trade on behalf of the individual.

3. Filling out the correct paperwork

There are several ways the appropriate paperwork can be filled. An individual can choose to order the paperwork by mail services. The other method will entail downloading the papers from the internet in the form of a PDF file. The next step will involve an individual checking the transaction charges by the bank for transferring funds to an individual's brokerage account. This fee is important because it affects the profit calculation in the Forex trade.

    4. Activation of the account

The most common occurrence entails the broker sending the activation link to an individual's email. The link sent always contains guidelines that help an individual to start.

Starting Trading

    1. Analysis of the market

Market analysis is always the first step while starting to trade in the Forex market. There are several ways an individual can use to analyze the market. They include:

    I. Technical analysis; technical analysis entails the use of chats or historical data. These forms will help a Forex trader to be able to predict the movement of currency basing his thought on the previous events. These data can be obtained from several sources. The main form sources include from the brokerage or the MetaTrader which is a common platform for those in the Forex trade.

    II. Fundamental analysis; this form of analysis involves taking a keen look at the key areas in a country's economy. The information got from these fundamental areas form a key to a person trading choices.

III. Sentimental analysis; this form of market analysis is highly subjective. An individual using this form of market analysis will try to get a good analysis of the market mood. This will enable an individual to know if the market is bullish. It is very difficult to put a finger on the sentiment of the market. However, an individual can be able to make very good guesses that influence his or her trade.

2. Determining an individual's margin

This is highly dependable on the broker's strategy in place. An individual can make investments of small amounts of money and still be able to make huge trades in the Forex market. An example can be used of an individual with a desire to trade one hundred units at one percent margin. This will make the broker put one thousand American dollars in an individual's account to act as security. If an individual makes the gains, it will add in his or her account to its value. On the other hand, loses will deduct from the individual's account from its value. Such occurrences have made individuals invest 2% of the funds in a specific pair currency.

3. Placing of an individual order

An individual at this point can place orders of various kinds. These orders include:

- Market order; this order includes an individual using the market order to instruct his or her broker to buy or sell at the present market rates.

- Limit orders; this point entails an individual instructing his or her broker to trade at a precise price. An individual can sell the currency when it lowers to a certain price or he or she can buy when it gains up to a certain price.
- Stop orders; this order involves two of the options. An individual can decide to buy currency above the present value in the market. On the other hand, an individual can choose to sell currency below the present market value.

4. Watching an individual's profit and loss

At this point, an individual is warned from becoming emotional. It is because the market is very volatile in most cases. An individual is predicted to observe lots of ups and downs. Therefore, one is supposed to be firm with his or her strategy in the market. This will enable him to see profits coming overtime if he or she is confident in his or her strategy.

Chapter 8 How to Find Undervalued Stocks

You need to perform three fundamental steps in order to find undervalued stocks:

1. Perform a preliminary evaluation of several stocks to see if they meet your investment criteria;

2. Based on your preliminary evaluation, develop a shortlist of stocks that you want to further examine and evaluate; and

3. Perform a more detailed investigation of your shortlisted stocks by closely inspecting the companies' financial information.

The internet has actually made it a lot easier for investors to acquire the free financial information of companies they are interested to invest in. There are many websites now such as Edgars and Sedar that offer extensive databases of financial data, including audited financial statements, press releases, corporate reports, stock prices, and earnings per share.

However, given the barrage of information, how will you know if a particular stock is currently being sold below its inherent worth? Here are just two of the financial ratios that you should look at to assess a particular stock's inherent worth:

- Price/Earnings (P/E) Ratio

You will soon hear financial analysts say that a particular stock is currently selling for "x-times earnings" – 20-times earnings or 10.5-times earnings. This means that the stock's current market price is currently selling at 20 times higher than the earnings per share of the company. The goal is to find stocks with very low P/E ratios because that means that those companies are selling their stocks at lower prices.

- Earnings Yield

Earnings yield is basically the opposite of P/E ratio. Therefore, a company with a 20-times earnings (P/E ratio) has a 1/20 or 5% earnings yield. If value investors are looking for low P/E ratios, the opposite applies with earnings yield (i.e. Value investors are looking for stocks with higher earnings yield compared to other companies within the same industry.).

In addition to the quantitative assessments mentioned above, you must also perform qualitative assessments that allow you to better understand the intrinsic value of a particular company.

One of these qualitative assessments is the review of the company's "insider purchasing activity." You want to know what the company's executives (senior managers, officers, directors and other major stockholders) are doing with their stock ownerships.

These insiders, especially the senior managers and the board of directors, have "inside" information about the operations of their own company. Therefore, if you see them aggressively buying their company's stock, you can reasonably presume that the company's operations are moving towards a favorable future.

However, don't jump to quick conclusions when you see an insider selling his or her stock ownership. It does not always mean that the company is heading towards bankruptcy or harder times. For all you know, that particular director or senior manager is in dire need of extra cash to fund his or her personal expenditures. You can, however, begin to doubt the company's future prospects if many of the insiders begin to sell most of their stock ownerships. When you observe that scenario, you need to perform further investigations to see if the company is heading towards difficult times.

Now, you may ask "How will I know when a company's board of directors or senior management is buying or selling their stocks?" Don't worry because the Securities and Exchange Commission (SEC) has made it easier for investors to know about this information. Insiders are obligated to report their purchasing activities to the SEC within 2 business days after the transaction. You can then freely access this information through the official SEC website.

The Essence of Value Investing

As we mentioned earlier, you need to have the eagerness to do some serious reading and investigations if you want to be successful in value investing.

You do not really need to have a degree in finance and accounting, but it will greatly help if you make the effort to learn about basic accounting so that you can more properly analyze and interpret financial statements. Remember that you do not make a decision to buy a particular stock because its financial ratios look promising or because you recently learned that its current market price has considerably dropped. In order to determine whether a particular stock is a good buy or not, you have to rely on more than simply taking in everything you see at face value. You will need to use your common sense and your critical thinking skills in order to be successful.

Beyond the financial ratios and the insider purchasing activity, you need to spend some time to ask the following questions and to find the answers:

· How do you think the company's operations will look like five years, ten years, or even twenty years from now?

· Will the company be able to continuously increase its revenues either by selling more or by increasing their prices?

· Will the company be able to sustain an efficient operation by making sure that costs of goods sold and operating expenses are strictly controlled?

· How often do they sell or close down divisions or subsidiaries that do not make any profit?

- How strong is the company within their industry? Are they one of the market leaders? Do they have stronger competitors?

As you become more experienced, you will know what other questions you need to ask. Once you have the answers, you use these together with the financial ratios and insider purchasing activities to determine whether a particular stock is a good buy or not. There is no specific formula that you can use so this is where you need to rely on your own common sense and critical thinking.

To improve your chances to succeed in value investing, it is advisable to purchase stocks from companies that you understand. This is the strategy that helped Warren Buffett earn millions from his stock investments. If you have always worked in the airline industry, you can say that you have a good working knowledge of that industry and the companies within it. Because you normally buy clothes, grocery items, and household appliances, you most probably have basic knowledge about the retail industry.

Another technique that successful value investors utilize is to purchase stocks of companies that have been producing products or rendering services for a long time and there is a very high probability that their products or services will continue to be in demand. You cannot identify these companies simply by reviewing their financial information. You will have to perform some critical thinking to determine which companies fall under this category. Let's take the Coca-Cola

Company as an example. Coke products have been widely accepted worldwide for several decades now and many people believe that these products will continue to be in demand for a very long time. You can look at other companies you are familiar with and see how they have adapted over time. It is also ideal if you can perform an analysis of the management style of the companies to see how effective their corporate governance is in ensuring that the companies can thrive during both good times and bad times.

Remember, value investors invest for the long-term; they do not make haphazard and random investment decisions. They take their time in reviewing and investigating a particular company before they use their capital to purchase stocks. It is never enough to just browse through the stock market prices and read quick commentaries from financial analysts.

Chapter 9 The Forex Candlestick

Candlesticks are great strategies to go with no matter what kind of trading you want to work with. They can really show you the trends that are going on in the market for that security, and you can adjust the methods to work no matter what kind of market you enter. There are actually quite a few different types of candlestick strategies that you can work with, and we will take a look at a few of them below:

The Double Top

This kind of candlestick pattern is going to form after there is either strong bullish conditions or a strong price rally. It is easy to define because of the double top patterns kind of looks like two mountain peaks that form into an "M" shape on your chart: An example of what you are looking for in your graphs when using the double top strategy includes:

These two peaks will generally show up because they are reacting to strong resistance that shows up in the market. the initial bullish wave is going to hit the point of resistance before it does a bounce right away. It can then find a bit of support again. Eventually, the bulls of the market are going to pick up their steam again. This results in the market pushing that stock up to a higher price. Then the market will be able to retest that resistance level. Often the bulls are not going to have enough strength to control the market for long and the price ends up doing a bounce again to help make that second peak.

The best way to trade when you see the double top candlestick pattern for the trader to watch some of the charts and wait to see that second peak start to form. Then you can do some price breaks that are short and happen below your neckline.

The Double Bottom

The next type of candlestick that you can use is known as the double bottom. This kind of candlestick pattern is the inverse of what we did with the double top pattern. It is going to form when you see a strong bearish move and it will have more of a "W" shape to it compared to the last one. An example of what this would look like in the market is the following:

A double bottom is going to signal there the bears of the market are exhausted. This gives the bulls time to take control at that support level. Now the bears of the market are able to move the prices so they go back down to the stocks support level. At some point, the bulls are going to try and drive that price back up. Because the bulls are rejecting this support, they are going to create that first V shape. The bears are going to work on fighting the bulls and driving the price of the stock back down.

When the bulls and bears fight and the market gets back to the support level that second time, the bulls are going to be the winners again, at least for a bit, and they work to drive the prices back up again. This results in another V in the chart. This final move will help finish this pattern.

Head and Shoulders

The head and shoulders strategy is another candlestick pattern that works on exhaustion. This one is not always the most reliable because it forms after the market has been trending in a certain direction for some time.

When the bulls start to try and gain some strength here and push the price of the security up again. The last resistance line that you tested on the chart is going to be broken through with this. But these higher prices are not ones that the bulls are able to keep with, and the price will go back under the resistance due to this false break. The false break is going to create the head part of this pattern.

With this pattern, the bulls are going to fail in their quest and they won't be able to maintain the prices that fall above your resistance level. When this happens, they are going to gain a little more strength, trying to accomplish this goal one more time. Your resistance is going to hold in this case and the price will then fall back to the support line that you have. This last phase is going to provide that second shoulder and will end this pattern. The containment line, which was the support during this whole process, is the neckline. An example of how this strategy is going to look in a chart is the following:

This pattern is hard to find because you may not be sure whether you are getting a double top or the head and shoulders, and you may miss out on some trades because you don't know what to expect. Most traders need to be in the market for some time before they can see this one working out. Treating it like the double top may be the best bet to help you earn a profit. But if you see that the "head" forms and goes way up and it has one shoulder ahead of it, you can get some relief knowing that there will be another raise on the second shoulder where you can make some profits as well.

The inverse head and shoulders

After some strong bearish activity, the market is going to hit its support and then it will retrace and find the resistance. This activity is going to help create the first phase or your left shoulder. Just like with the regular head and shoulders option, it is hard to tell whether the inverted head and shoulders pattern is forming when you reach this first part.

After this happens, the bears will push the market down. This causes a false break, or a breakout trap, that is below the support that you already tested. When the price then shoots back up above the support, you will have the head section of this pattern form.

Next, the bulls are going to retest your support levels. At this point, the support will hold and the price is going to bounce back to the neckline of this pattern. This will end the pattern for inverted head and shoulders. The classic way that you can trade with this method is to just wait out the market and see when it pushes above this neckline. Then it is a good time to do a long trade. An example of how this is going to look when you see it on one of your graphs includes:

Squeeze Patterns

The next type of candlestick pattern that you may see is known as a squeeze pattern. Wedges are going to form any time that the market stalls because there is a period of indecision for that security. Then the market will start producing higher lows and lower highs on a consistent basis. This pattern is then going to compress itself into the tip of the wedge before the market ends up in a breakout pattern.

Once the price for that security reaches the tip of the wedge, there is a big chance that a breakout is going to occur. It is possible for a wedge to be bilateral. This means that the breakout you see could go in either direction. You need to have a good idea of the market and how that security has been doing to figure out whether you will see a breakout that goes up or down.

The classic method that you will use in order to trade these wedge breaks is to buy breakouts at the top of the wedge, and then sell it when the price breakdown below the wedge.

These are a few of the different candlestick strategies that you can use when you are working in the forex market. Many people like to use candlesticks because they can really help show how strong or weak a trend is and there are options of strategies that work no matter how the market is doing. If you are still looking for the strategy you want to use with forex trading, you may need to consider one of these candlestick methods because they are easy to use and great for beginners who are just getting into the market.

Chapter 10 Stocks which need a growing economy to make money

There are certain stocks that only thrive during boom periods. As such, when consumers no longer have any excess funds to spend on things that aren't considered "necessities", these stocks are the ones often hit the hardest. If you have these in your portfolio, this isn't necessarily an indication to get rid of them, but their exposure should be hedged at the very least and I recommend making portfolio readjustments based on this.

Airlines

Airline stocks traditionally do terribly during recessions. Recreational air travel is something many people cut back on during the lean years. International and domestic vacations both get hit hard, as do the share prices of the major carriers. In addition, it's an industry with very high fixed costs which doesn't benefit from the recession in the slightest. It should be noted that discount carriers are less at risk as their model is always to keep prices low and make it up on the backend with extras.

It's estimated that airlines won't be hit as hard during the next recession due to industry consolidation. This has been happening ever since the deregulation of airlines in 1978 and we've gone from having over 400 carriers in the US to just 68 today with the big 4 (American, Southwest, Delta and United) making up around 70% of the market. Holding a large percentage of your portfolio in airline stocks is still not a great move though

Restaurants

Eating out is another big cut back from consumers during periods of economic downturn. The hardest hit is often the low to mid range casual dining chains that focus less on alcohol and more on food. Chains like P.F. Chang's, Red Robin are ones to watch.

Once again, the bargain chains are less prone to market conditions.

So don't go dumping your McDonald's stock yet (it could be argued that McDonald's are in the real estate business and not the restaurant business as it is). Takeout businesses like Dominoes Pizza are also less affected because their convenience model is one that still holds strong during bad times.

High end luxury items

Stocks that fall under this umbrella would be ones like Apple and GoPro, those that sell technological luxury with high price tags. Although people still buy these goods during lean years, they tend to delay their purchases and therefore the balance sheets of these companies don't look as good, causing the share prices to fall. On average, people replace their phones every 2 years for example, if they delay this to 3 years, this makes a significant impact on Apple's bottom line during a recession.

Another example of this would be Nike. If Nike customers decide they can wait another 6 months for a new pair of sneakers, this sends ripples throughout the company and in turn, leads to lower share prices. Some of the larger companies may be able to mitigate some of the risk through their international operations, but the US numbers will still drag their prices down during bad periods.

Chapter 11 *Diversification*

Diversification is a very important strategy for investing. As a financial term, it means simply distributing your investments in various industries for stocks, combining different financial assets, and creating a mix of these assets that will enable you to meet your investment goals. But in the world of investing, diversification refers to a very specific strategy of investment—the careful selection of assets that would react in different ways to a particular event. So far, we have identified the events that create market volatility and make investing in the stock market a risky endeavor. A portfolio combines shares with ETFs, REITs, trust funds, bonds, and other assets, but if not done properly, it can combine assets that react the same way or in a similar manner to events in the economy.

With diversification, you put together stocks that fit together like a cogwheel so that every drop in the price of a particular asset is counterbalanced by a rise in the value of another. When the price of oil stocks goes up, you can almost be assured that airlines, which have to charge more because oil is selling at higher prices, will be doing less business. Their stocks will most probably drop. The inverse is also very true. Having a stock from each sector in your stock portfolio means that your portfolio will always be balanced out whatever happens in either industry. If the oil and airlines industries combination does not appeal to you, then you can trade out oil with railway companies. When anything happens to reduce traveler confidence in the airline industry, railroads experience a surge in travelers and vice versa.

Another fantastic combination of assets that can help you keep your portfolio balanced out is that of stocks and bonds in general terms. Stocks normally drop in price when interest rates climb, a time when the price of bonds climbs. Most investment gurus define diversification as simply ensuring that you don't keep all your eggs in a single basket. This hypothetical basket represents the geographical location, economic sector, and investment type.

Pros and Cons

The benefits of diversification have been addressed at length above. The main reason why we diversify, however, is that it allows you to secure your investments against market volatility and keep your investment stable.

Another advantage of diversification is that it allows us to cover our bases. By thinking about the risk quotient of assets before choosing to invest in them, we can identify potential hurdles before they become too problematic. For one thing, diversification forces us to think about our risk tolerance, which is the foundation for a good portfolio.

One of the biggest drawbacks to diversification comes from a very curious aspect of the diversification process—choosing your assets. With so many assets to choose from, you might get stumped, unable to choose between different assets.

Another disadvantage of diversification is that it demands that you select stocks from different, unrelated industries. Choosing between a few different good assets in the same market sector leaves the chance that the asset you forfeit is the best one of them all and you can only watch as it rises in price and you cannot take advantage. The opportunity cost of choosing one stock over another could be very demoralizing.

Another con to excessive diversification is that the balancing out of assets in your portfolio whereby a rise in one asset is met by a corresponding drop in another leads to average returns. The cost of trying too hard to ensure that your portfolio will bring you no losses is the fact that you can never make much money. The former hinders the latter.

Another drawback to diversification is that you are more likely to incur massive costs while trying to balance it out by constantly buying and selling.

So is it worthwhile diversifying?

The answer is *definitely!* A diversified portfolio is a huge confidence booster because it assures you that your investment is secure. The only problems arise when you overly diversify or micromanage the risks associated with every asset on your portfolio. Diversification goes hand in hand with portfolio management. The more closely you monitor your portfolio, the better you can diversify. If you think the passive style of portfolio management does not pay enough attention to the assets in your portfolio, a midway point between active and passive portfolio management can allow you to hit the sweet spot between over-diversifying and not doing it thoroughly enough.

Chapter 12 Money management

The amount of money one makes in trading is solely dependent on the time they spend on the market. This is a major motivating factor since there are times when some stocks are selling lower and gaining more. Therefore, when a beginner starts identifying what protocols they should use in trading, eventually they start to reap in some profits.

The essence of these profits, however, is not to buy the latest trends and keep up with the most advanced technology. When managed properly, these profits can make even the most trivial of rookies into a dignified millionaire.

This skill set of money management is important in the fact that it entails managing risks and leverage. This allows the trader to last longer in the market without burning out.

The greatest danger lies in the leverage part.

There are a few things to consider, therefore in the whole process so as to achieve results:

> 1. Trade only the stocks that have a promising risk/reward ratio. This is where you compare what loses you will incur as opposed to the profits on the stock. This ratio then should be at 3:1 with the profits being on the higher end so as to avoid an account blow up. This is one

of the calculations you make while entering and exiting the forex market. Most traders assume this fact and end up regretting later on. You have to evaluate all the possible outcomes in a trade. You can never be having 100% guarantees that you will encounter a loss or a profit. However, you can have predictions in which the ratio shows that there is a high likelihood of trade moving in a given direction. Depending on the ratio, you can easily tell if an investment is worth taking or if you should avoid engaging in it at all costs.

These numbers are not difficult to establish. There are certain pointers that will show you if you are wasting your time, or if it is a worthy investment. Such is essential in helping you make the right choices that can give you what you want. Instead of fully depending on luck to get your profits, it is good to get the facts right. The graphs and charts available in the forex market can help in coming up with some of these figures. You only need to keenly note how they move and come up with an appropriate ratio on how the trade is likely to move.

2. Set your trading platform to have a Max Dollar Stop-Loss. Sometimes, even seasoned traders are lured into making trades that eventually hurt the account due to eagerness. By having this limitation set, the rookie is able to avoid sudden moves on his account that might result in tragedy. This

max dollar amount must help the trader sustain an 80% profit/loss margin. We tend to have huge expectations of increasing our earnings, and this can result in greed. You find that an investor keeps trading multiple times so that they can double their profits. This move results in overtrading, which is, at times challenging for an individual. To avoid this, ensure that you know when to exit a trade. This is a discipline that most people lack. You find that they keep engaging in trade without placing much thought and consideration into what they are doing. In the end, this issue bounces back to them, and they end up making huge losses.

A max dollar stop loss creates a limit for traders. It prevents them from engaging in more trades than they can handle in a day. This strategy helps them in minimizing potential losses and helps in boosting their earnings. At times you find that investors make losses in several trades, but they keep trading with the expectations that the next trade may earn a profit. That is more like gambling with luck, and the cards may work on your favor, or they may fail. If it happens that they keep losing in the other trades, the loss incurred will be huge, and they will not be able to recover from it.

3. While going for a loss, stick to a considerable limit. With day trading, as the exit hours near, people tend to get desperate and

average down considerably. Use this chance to survive with your account by making your selling price a considerable amount to what you bought it for so as to avoid huge losses. This selling point also has the advantage to culminate into a profit-making venture. Making the right call is a huge challenge in options trading. Your daily decisions will determine the kind of trader that you will become. In life, we are faced with major challenges, and it is the decision that we make that allows us to win or lose our battles.

When you decide to go to a casino, you have high expectations that you will win in the various games that you engage in. This thought crosses everyone else that heads there. You find that everyone hopes that they will emerge a winner. The sad truth is, there can never be two winners, one party has to lose as the other party walks home with a lot of cash. As you gamble, you have to be open to the fact that you can either go home with a loss or a profit. Either way, it all depends on luck on that particular day and how tactical you were while playing.

This also applies to options trading. There are some tough decisions that you will have to make; like being open to the fact that you can get a loss at any time.

4. Time our actions in order to make rational judgments on the stocks. This will allow you to calculate your moves without being rushed and thus avoiding losses. This is also

important when playing into a scene that will escalate into making profits. Each and every move that you make while trading options has to be well calculated. With the knowledge of the various options strategies, it gets easier to do this. You are probably wondering why I keep insisting on the options strategies. Well, they are the foundation of prosperous trades. You have to makes sure that you are well aware of all the option strategies at your disposal if you intend to be an expert trader. These are the tricks that ensure if you will walk away with a win or if you will end up regretting the choices that you made.

For instance, we can evaluate the situation of players engaging in American football. It's a tough game, but a good strategy is what differentiates a loser from a winner. There are a lot of decisions to be made on the field. These decisions determine if a team will emerge a winner or a loser. The winning team usually has the right strategy and makes the right calls while playing the game.

This strategy also applies in day trading. A trader needs to know when to engage in a trade and when to avoid getting in a trade.

5. If the trade involves a higher risk, avoid it. At a point when one would be making losses, it is often observed that traders make hasty decisions and acquire more stocks in order to cover their losses. This is a tricky move as there is the risk of acquiring illiquid stocks or

even run down stocks which will burn the trader. The beginner needs to understand that losses are made so as to learn where not to go the next time, and that time should be given to improve the stocks. Observe the patterns and avoid these high-risk trades.

Part of trading involves analyzing the charts and graphs in the forex market. The information acquired from these graphs is essential in knowing how the market moves. It acts as a pointer in knowing the right direction and way of doing things. Some of the trade moves that investors make are made with the intention of earning profits. At times, it turns out that they make the wrong call and end up regretting the actions that they made. The choices made by a trader count a lot while trading options.

These choices determine if they will earn a profit or make a tremendous loss.

Two wrongs can never make a right. We have had traders engage in a trade with the aim of compensating a previous loss. This may appear as a strong move to make, but it can result in a loss in the long run. You will be surprised that even after incurring another loss, some traders will still try making another trade which could end up in another loss. We have to make the right decisions while trading options and we should not expect too much within a short duration of time. Some efforts are required if we aim at being expert traders.

Chapter 13 Mindset and Psychology

Traders must have a certain mindset when it comes to investing. Investing in stock takes a lot of self-discipline. There is a certain psychology that traders must become familiar with to be successful in their investments. There is a whole investing mindset that must be utilized to drive results. Investors must detach themselves from their emotions when investing in stock; otherwise, they risk trading out of fear and greed. Investors must also not become too attached to any stock. Although there is an art to investing, it is important that investors utilize logic to drive their actions.

Self-Discipline

Self-discipline is crucial when it comes to investing. Investors must be able to follow their plans and achieve their goals. However, many investors become tempted by the idea of better performance and abandon all logic in hopes of achieving greater returns on their investments. They will use emotions when it comes to market conditions. They may also incur greater costs because of a lack of discipline. Investors must stick with their original plan despite temptations otherwise. A short-term sacrifice will be worth it in the long-term. Although it may not be the most appealing path, the disciplined path is most often the most successful path, especially when it comes to trading.

Following the original plan and goals that the investor set is crucial. Although there are situations in which it may be more beneficial to adjust the plans due to a highly changing market or personal financial misfortune, it is better to stick to the original plan most of the time. Once the investor strays from the path originally, it will become easier to repeat that action and abandon all original plans. The investor may act without using logic and end up incurring great losses. When this happens, however, investors fail to see the consequences of their actions in the long-term. Stocks that the investors should have held onto could have resulted in gains, but the investor chose to incur losses because of a lack of discipline instead. The investor opens themselves up to allowing for loopholes whenever they deem necessary, and they hurt themselves in the long-term. The investor should create a plan for what to do if the market is negative and stick to this. They should create this plan beforehand so that they are not biased at all. However, the real discipline is actually following through with this plan when the time comes.

The investor should also be disciplined in their amount of investments. Instead of deciding last-minute use the money that they planned to set aside for stock on spending, they should stick to the original plan. It is quite easy to say that one will not invest this week and get right back to it the next week, but they have already fallen off of the plan. This can discourage the investor and lead to further lack of discipline in the future. The best way to avoid this from happening is to stick with the plan in the first place. The investor must stick with the plans for both buying and selling. They must not sell stocks that they didn't originally plan to, and they must also buy stocks that they did plan to. Regardless of market activity, the investor should still stick to their investing goals. Instead of holding back on new investments, the investor should stick to their original plan. Good habits must be formed, and the investor must not slack off despite possible obstacles. For some activities, flexibility is important. For stock, though, sticking to the plan is much more important for ensuring success.

The investor must not change their portfolio based on recent market activities. This can prove to be quite difficult, especially in a bear market. However, it is usually worth it to stick through the hard times and wait for another period of growth. One's portfolio should be managed and properly rebalanced as necessary. Although it may be tempting to change this based on market conditions, the investor must hold out through the rough times. If investing for the long-term, the investor must ensure that the investments are, indeed, kept for the long-term.

Trading Psychology

The psychology that goes into trading encompasses several factors. The trader must be able to control their emotions, make quick decisions, and remain disciplined. Of course, this is in addition to being able to understand companies and predict the direction in which the stock will go. With enough practice and research, anyone can master the technical side of trading. It's those who master the psychological side that is truly successful in trading. This is what separates the good traders from the great traders. Trading psychology can be a skill crafted by practice, but it also requires the trader to shift their way of thinking.

Traders must understand the emotions that go into trading. By first understanding them, they will allow themselves to become more skillful in the way they handle such emotions. Traders must realize that fear is a natural response to bad news about the stock market. It is natural that traders will feel a sense of urgency and be tempted to liquidate their holdings, reduce risk, or otherwise sell their stocks. This, at the time, seems to be a wise move. However, traders must make decisions quickly that will benefit them in the long term, not satisfy their emotions in the short-term. By doing so, they may risk losses, but they will not miss out on the gains that they otherwise would miss out on had they given in to their emotions. It is important for traders to realize that fear stems from what people believe is a threat to them. In this instance, the threat is to their money. Traders must recognize what is making them fearful and what the best way of dealing with that fear is. It is important to come up with a plan for what to do in hypothetical scenarios before they actually occur. What is the best way to deal with a certain outcome of stock x? Traders must answer such questions before they occur so that they have a logical look at the situation. If they wait until it actually occurs, their minds will be foggy due to the emotions they feel. They may also change the way they perceive such occurrences. Instead of viewing a drop in the price of the stock as a loss, it may be viewed as a temporary dip before further growth will occur. This shift of mindset is crucial for adopting positive trading habits.

In addition to overcoming fear, investors must know how to overcome greed. If an investor holds onto a winning stock for too long, trying to get every possible amount of money they can, these gains may quickly turn to losses. Holding onto a stock for too long can prove to be less profitable than one may imagine. Yet again, traders must come up with a plan ahead of time. They must know when the right time to let go of a stock is. At the time, it seems like a wise move to the investor. They may earn more, do better than they originally thought, and make more gains. This sometimes occurs. Most of the time, however, greed is not the right choice. Traders must distinguish between greed and making wise decisions based on market changes. Sometimes, it is better to stray from the original plan. What often occurs, however, is that emotion interferes with logic, and the investor makes an unwise move by listening to their heart instead of their head.

Investors must create an extensive plan and set rules for themselves. Instead of "going with the flow," it's important to have a step-by-step plan for the investor's trading endeavors. This should be based on rational decisions, not spur-of-the-moment emotions or instincts. They must plan out when they will enter a trade and when they will exit a trade. This must be followed no matter what, and this is a great way to eliminate emotional bias. The trader may plan for certain occurrences. If unpredictable earnings occur, whether positive or negative, the trader may establish exceptions to their plan should these occur. The trader may buy a security if certain macroeconomic events occur. They may also set limits to eliminate fear and greed. These should be upper and lower limits. The upper limits will eliminate greed, and the lower will limit fear. If such a limit is reached, the trader may stop their activities for the day to eliminate emotions from taking over their activities.

Traders must also not let regret get in the way. What is in the past is in the past. It is beneficial to recognize potential mistakes, but they should not get in the way of one's performance. Perhaps the trader regrets keeping their investment for the time period that they did. Perhaps they regret the stocks that they chose. No matter what the trader could have done, it does not matter. What matters is that they use this knowledge to improve themselves in the future. This means that the next time, they may conduct more research than they did this time.

On the other hand, traders should not rationalize their mistakes. Although it is important to not dwell on the past and all of the possible ways that the trader messed up in, the trader should still recognize that they made mistakes. This is important for self-improvement, as there will always be ways in which the trader could have conducted their trades more efficiently or effectively. As a result, the trader should definitely analyze what did go wrong every time period that they wish to do so. This will make the trader better and improve their future performance and decision-making skills.

Investing Mindset

Traders may also learn different mindsets from other traders. By researching extensively and hearing how other people conduct their trades, there is much to learn. By increasing knowledge, the investor may decrease their negative emotional reactions. They will further understand the stock market and how it operates, and this will help to eliminate such reactions.

Although it is important to stick to one's plan, traders must adopt flexible mindsets. They must be willing to try new tools, buy and sell new stocks, research new companies, and trade differently. There is no "correct" way to trade. There are simply many different ways of doing so. Some may be more profitable than others. Some may work well for one trader and not well for another. Traders should be willing to slightly experiment to see what the best way for them to trade is. This may also decrease emotion when it comes to stock.

Investors should also be critical of themselves and view their trading from a logical stance. There will be certain ways to trade that will result in greater returns. Traders must be willing to reflect on their performance and see what resulted in gains and what didn't. There is always room for improvement, and traders must recognize that. Perhaps for one time period, the trader wasn't researching as thoroughly and missed certain aspects that they should have spent more time on. Perhaps the trader did let emotion influence their trades. By recognizing potential bad habits, the trader will be able to work on improving themselves and making themselves a more profitable and skillful trader for the future.

Traders must use technical analysis to drive their investing decisions. There are various ways of doing so. Perhaps the trader wishes to focus on charts. This can prove highly beneficial for seeing a visual representation of performance. The trader may have a group of investors that they seek advice from with their trades. They may have a journal to write their plan in. There are programs to use to help with investments. Whichever way the trader prefers that they conduct their business, there should be some sort of support to help logically analyze their decisions. There must be a guide.

Patience is also crucial for traders. Fear and greed, combined with a lack of patience, can truly harm the trader's ability to think quickly and make the right decision. By practicing patience, the trader will be able to decide better when the right time for buying or selling a stock is. Otherwise, the trader might be willing to jump into or out of the market despite the bad timing of doing so. Practicing patience can improve one's ability to time the market better and hold onto investments that will perform better with time while letting go of investments that have had their time.

Detaching Emotion from Stock

Emotions and trading simply don't mix. In addition to greed and fear, traders must be willing not to get attached to their stocks. Stock investments will constantly change. There will be times where it is the wisest move to invest in one stock and not another. However, traders will often become quite attached to a particular stock. The investor must be able to let go of stocks that simply aren't beneficial for them to hold on to. There is no guarantee for how well a stock will perform, as the market is constantly changing, and stocks will change, too. Investors must separate themselves from their stocks and learn when to let a particular stock go.

When trading, it is important to separate logic from emotion. Trading is a numbers game. It's all about what will benefit the trader in the long-term. While it may be easy to let fear or greed take over, to let one's mistakes hinder their future performance, or to become attached to a particular stock, these are not beneficial for one's performance. The trader must adopt a certain mindset and familiarize themselves with the proper psychology of trading. Doing so will prove highly beneficial to the trader.

Chapter 14 Risk Management

The stock market is one of the most rewarding passive investments you can make; you could double your principal within seven years! As indicated in the chart below, the stocks in the S&P 500 have appreciated over 100 times since 1900 (data is purely illustrative).

But where there is a reward, there is also a risk. It is also very possible for you to lose money, which is why you need to be very careful how you pick your stocks and manage them. But you will soon find that there are some risks that you can keep under control and others that are totally out of your control. The only thing you can do in the face of uncontrollable risks is to safeguard your investment against massive losses. And because every investor is always keenly observing the market to spot possible future danger and make a move right now to avoid it, the riskier a situation looks, the more likely it is that a bunch of investors will react to it in a certain way. The concerted actions of investors affect the stock market in a particular manner, which brings about price volatility.

Stock Market Volatility

Risk in the stock market is caused by interest rates, equity prices, foreign exchange rates, and commodity prices. A higher interest rate makes it more expensive to borrow money for both businesses and consumers, slowing down economic activity. Bonds are also affected by the prevailing interest rate in an economy, but in the inverse direction. Higher interest rates drive down demand for bonds and cause an overall lag in the trading volumes of the stock market. As for stocks, the interest rate affects not just the performance of listed companies; it influences the ability of the public and brokerage firms to deal in leveraged stock purchases. A higher interest rate, therefore, spells doom for the whole stock market.

Price risk comes from the volatility of stocks. It is the probability that the price of a stock or stocks in an investment portfolio will fall over a long period of time. The risk of a stock dropping in price can either be systematic or unsystematic. Systematic risk is the risk that occurs across the whole stock market, bringing down the price of stocks in many or all sectors of the economy. Unsystematic risk, on the other hand, affects a single stock or the stocks in a particular industry, like the oil and gas sector when oil prices drop.

The foreign exchange risk affects the price of stocks indirectly through the company whose stock an investor owns. It also affects the profitability of the stock portfolio when it contains a few foreign stocks. The price at which currencies exchange shifts based on the economic performance of that country. Companies that have foreign operations and move profits home after making them in another country are affected by the exchange rate in bringing these profits back home. When the US currency gets stronger, the conversion of profits earned turns up less money, with the stock market responding by showing less enthusiasm with the company's shares, which brings its price down. For the diversified investor with foreign stocks, any profits earned in another country will still need to be transferred home. If the exchange rate changes for the worse, the return you will make will be considerably lower.

Finally, we have commodity risk, which is the unpredictability of the price of shares that is caused by the changing cost of commodities, such as oil, minerals, agricultural produce, etc. The stocks of companies that are directly involved in the industry of an affected commodity will experience the biggest bump in prices. For example, if beef prices rise steeply in the open market, the profit margins of food companies, such as McDonald's, will fall immediately because investors can foretell lower profit margins in six months or one year. When oil prices climb, it becomes more expensive to transport goods, which means that retailers will hike prices, see considerably fewer sales, and post less impressive financial reports sometime later. Anticipating this poor performance, investors will sell, bringing the stock price down. The good thing about commodity risk is that it is very easy not just to mitigate it but also to profit from this risk. While transportation companies and those that rely on them to do business suffer, oil companies will be outperf0rming their peers. These stocks move in opposite directions with a particular product as the fulcrum balances each other out.

As indicated above, you can neither predict nor control risk. The best you can hope for is to hedge against total loss by maintaining a well-hedged portfolio. With risk comes volatility, which is essentially the rise and fall of stock prices from time to time as investors react to the goings-on.

The foremost cause of risk in the stock market and the volatility that accompanies it is the economy, to which the stock market is inextricably linked. Any downturns in the economy create a corresponding decline in stock market performance. For example, after the economy lost trillions in the dot-com bubble between 2000 and 2002, the stock market went into decline, with all major indexes dropping by significant levels. What happens when the economy is bad is that there isn't as much money for people to invest in stocks anymore. The demand drops—meaning, stock prices fall. People who already own shares, therefore, lose a significant portion of their investment. Even worse, the losses suffered during an economic downturn take time to recover as the stock market adjusts back to its previous position. Not only do you lose money as an investor, but you also lose valuable time when your investment is recovering loses instead of accumulating gains. Foreign stocks come in handy in enabling you to mitigate against risks caused by a downturn in the domestic economy.

Inflation erodes the purchasing power of the currency and eats into any cash reserves a person may hold. Fixed-interest investments, like bonds, are most affected by inflation because unlike stocks, they do not benefit from price adjustments companies do when inflation rises. Whatever the percentage gain an investment provides, the percentage of inflation eats directly into that, so that an investment that produces an interest of, say, 4.5% at 2% inflation gives the investor effective capital gains of 2.5%. The higher the inflation rate, the lower the effective interest rate of an investment becomes. To make matters worse for the stock market, inflation also affects other sectors of the economy. A recession is often preceded by high inflation levels. It causes stocks to rise in price, but it also creates massive volatility.

The stock market is a perfect study in human psychology. When a stock performs well, people flock to buy it, causing the price to shoot up even higher and adding to the belief that it is an attractive investment opportunity. This phenomenon is referred to as market value risk. Everyone wants to be in on the next biggest thing, which creates sort of a herd mentality. Trends in the market determine which sector of the economy investors flock and, for that matter, the specific stocks they prefer to buy. Especially when you buy the stock of a company considered as boring and unexciting, you will be exposed to market value risk, with minimal investor interest bringing the value of your stock down and taking a huge chunk off your investment. Market value risk would be a nonentity if it weren't so hard to watch the rest of the stock market growing while your stock flat-lines. In fact, for many seasoned investors, the pains of market value risk present a great opportunity to consolidate their holding in a company.

But many investors have also fallen to the temptation to sell and join the rest of the hoi polloi in chasing the next big thing. Spreading your money in a few stocks in different sectors gives you the relief of having at least one stock that is doing well at any one time.

The world economy is now more connected than ever. Any time a major economic power suffers a downturn in its economy, other economies feel it too. This is true even for rivals that have little political and cultural cooperation otherwise. China, for example, is a rival to the United States in practically every area, from financial system (communist versus capitalist) to information and media policies (highly controlled versus free press and information access). The two countries can hardly be called allies. But the economic codependency of the two countries means that any time the Chinese economy slows down, the stock market in America reacts. Case in point, the tariff wars that have been instigated by President Trump have been cited by pundits as one of the reasons why the stock market seems to have slowed down from its bull run that started with the election of Donald Trump. Geopolitics pretty much shape world stability. When Britain votes to leave the European Union, the region becomes considerably weaker as an economic bloc, which means strategic planning by international companies is affected. The stock market suffers. Any maneuverings by hostile world powers against any major military superpower are interpreted by the market as being a possible trigger for war. The stock market suffers.

At the individual stock level, the perception of the public about the state of its issuer is what causes volatility. The job of maintaining a good image in public is very crucial to any traded company. Public relations departments work around the clock to craft an image of their company that is appealing. Any hits and misses in the public relations department, especially for the "hot" shares that everyone is always keenly following, have an immediate effect on the stock price. The news media also contributes to this volatility. When a company is reported to have recalled a product, missed a product release date, suffered a data breach, or suffered any such misfortune, stock prices react instantly.

Risk does not come exclusively from external factors. Sometimes the reason why you lose a lot of money is simply that you were too afraid of losing it to start with. Most of the best investment opportunities you are ever going to find will come accompanied with massive risk. If you cannot overcome your fears and go through with an investment even if there is a chance your stock will drop and lose you some money, you will make "safe" investments in bonds and maybe preferred stocks, where you are assured of getting some returns. In 20 years, you will have doubled your initial investment. Had you taken a little more risk, you could have recouped it three times over or at least two times over if you account for possible losses in the 20-year investment period.

Risk Tolerance

To demonstrate the concept of risk tolerance, let's look at two examples. Richard is a 52-year-old corporate lawyer at a small firm in New Jersey. He has a small family of four, but he is the only breadwinner. With an eye in his life after retirement, he has invested in the stock market for the past 23 years and accumulated quite a fortune on his investment portfolio. And as a seasoned investor, he has seen it all. In fact, he barely made it through Black Monday. The lessons he learned then enabled him to sail easy over the dot-com bubble—even make some money on it. Byron is a 31-year-old programmer from Seattle. He is recently married, with two kids. Both he and his wife are gainfully employed. He is also mindful of the future and intends to invest well and hopefully retire early.

The year is 2008, and the stock market is in a panic because the banking industry is in a crisis. Normally, the seasoned, confident investor would be unshaken by this. After all, he has lived through it all. He knows how to work the ropes. The inexperienced investor is more likely to make a cautionary move. But in our special case, Richard systematically sells his high-interest shareholdings and puts the money in the lesser reward bonds market. Byron, the unseasoned investor, studies the market, makes a few strategically placed purchases, and three years later emerges with almost double the principal.

What does our little anecdote reveal about investing in the stock market? It shows that any two investors cannot stomach the same magnitude of risk. Even in the same conditions, with the same opportunities and risks, people will react differently to changes in the stock market. The man who is close to retirement, with his whole life's worth of investments at stake three years to his retirement date, can tolerate a lot less risk than a fresh-faced investor with his whole life ahead of him. To put it plainly, risk tolerance is the magnitude of risk that any investor can tolerate.

Some of the factors that affect risk tolerance include the time you have to keep investing, future work prospects, assets owned apart from stocks, social security funds, and the availability of endowments (e.g., inheritance and trust funds). People who have more of all these things tend to be more aggressive in their investments than those who have little of it. Another reason why an investor might be more aggressive in the face of massive risk is if they are well-versed in the art of investing. With years of investing under the belt, professional investors can invest in stocks that have a risk factor of 50–100% and a similar potential for return without blinking an eye. But even these investors are usually covered by a foundation of carefully accumulated risk-free portfolios.

In the hierarchy of risk tolerance, the daredevils who actively pursue high-risk and high-reward stocks are followed by people with a moderate tolerance for risk. The riskiest stocks moderate risk-takers will accept have a factor of 50%. A diversified stock portfolio comes in handy for people who have moderate risk tolerance.

At the very bottom of risk tolerance is the conservative investor. Conservative investors have virtually no tolerance for risk because the stakes for losing the accumulated gains are higher than those of losing out on a good return. Retirees like Richard fall in this category. The priorities change from the rate of return to liquidity and guarantee for returns.

Assessing Your Risk Tolerance
Each one of us has a different level of risk tolerance. To assess your risk tolerance, answer the following questions.

What are my goals? Investing is most effective when you have a perfect idea of what you are accumulating money for. It is even better when you have a solid idea exactly how much money you are going to need or at least a fairly accurate estimate. Based on goals alone, the more the money you need to attain a particular goal, the lesser the risk tolerance you can withstand, because it is better to have a fraction of the money you need to achieve a certain goal than lose all your money. With a properly formulated investment strategy and well-defined tolerance for risk, you can then proceed to invest prudently and hopefully make enough money to meet your goals.

How much time do I have? The timeline between starting your investment journey and the time when you would like to reap the rewards of your investment is very influential in determining the level of risk tolerance you can withstand. A longer timeline means that you can ride out the most volatile upturns and downturns in the market. The stock market recovers from the roughest of recessions in four or five years. For example, after the 2008 stock market crash, the market had completely recovered by 2014. An investor with a portfolio set to be liquidated in 2019 would have had ten years to recover while one who anticipated liquidating their portfolio in 2010 would have had much less time. As you move closer to the time you intend to liquidate your investment, your risk tolerance decreases considerably. This is because, on the one hand, you have probably already made all the money you anticipated and also because the stakes are higher with shorter timelines. Losing some returns from a 90% mature stock portfolio would hurt much worse than one that still has 50% of its timeline to make gains.

What is my life stage? The stage you are in life determines the amount of risk you can take. Older people with less time left in their working lives have less risk tolerance than younger people who have yet a lot more time to make more money and invest.

What is the size of my portfolio? A portfolio that holds $1 million can cushion a loss better than one worth $100,000. As long as the risks are spread around, people with bigger portfolios usually have a higher level of risk tolerance. Investors like Warren Buffett devote millions to each stock investment because he will hardly feel it if a few hundred thousand dollars is lost.

What is my personal comfort level? Some people are naturally risk-takers while others prefer to stick to the safer route. One way to determine your comfort level as far as the stock market goes is to participate in a mock trading exercise and see how stressed you are when your mock investment is performing badly. If you cannot stand to watch your money diminish as stock prices drop, then you should probably stick to the less uncertain areas of the stock market (e.g., bonds).

The Dangers of Ignoring Risk Tolerance
Before investing, it is very important that you determine your risk tolerance. Not only should you determine how much risk you can stand, but but you should also make sure that you have it written down somewhere you are not likely to forget. When you start investing, every investment should be confined to within the safest bounds of your risk tolerance. You can lose your money on nearly every kind of investment, but the levels of risk vary from one asset to another and from stock to stock. When you don't factor in your risk tolerance, you are likely to panic and exit from an investment when it is within your risk levels and possibly lose money when it picks up.

Investing requires a certain level of confidence that you cannot achieve without understanding your own risk tolerance. Finding out exactly what your risk tolerance is will give you a proper idea of the kinds of drops in share price you can stomach based on solid considerations discussed above. Even if you are less of a risk-taker, understanding the reasonable levels of risk tolerance suitable for someone with your financial goals, timeline, and portfolio size can embolden you to venture to the riskier sectors where rewards are higher. Similarly, an avid risk-taker will be cautioned by the results of their risk assessment to engage in less risky investments if they are not in a good stage in life for it.

Stock Portfolios

A stock portfolio is an investment tool that allows an investor to put together a collection of assets (e.g., stocks, bonds, mutual funds, ETFs, and commodities). A portfolio is usually a binder, physical or electronic, that is kept in the custody of the owner or placed with a portfolio management firm. The assets placed in the portfolio should be selected according to the investor's risk tolerance, a summary of which should also be kept with the portfolio as an electronic file or print-out.

The consideration for risk tolerance allows the investor to update their portfolio by selling off any assets that no longer align with their investment goals, keeping the portfolio true to their aims and objectives. So if your risk tolerance is high, your investment style will be aggressive, which calls for a different mix of high- and low-risk assets from the conservative style of investment. If you want the best of both worlds, you can go with a balanced portfolio. From the word go, your portfolio should reflect your investment style.

When planning out your portfolio, it helps to think of it as a pie that you can cut into smaller pieces of different sizes. Every piece of the pie represents a class of assets in which you invest to reach a certain goal. Even when considering risk tolerance and other such matters, portfolio breakdown should be done in accordance with the investment objectives and keeping in mind the amount of money you have to invest. For example, if you are starting out with savings of $100,000, you may not want to invest it all in one stock or in stocks only. You also want to be sure that the way you distribute your money among the different asset types will give you the returns you need to meet your goals.

As a rule of thumb, the stocks of small-cap companies with high growth potential serve as the foundation for high-risk tolerance portfolios. These stocks may grow over 100% in a few years, but they are also just as likely to collapse and lead to a huge loss. Other high-reward and high-risk assets include large-cap growth stocks, real estate investment trusts, and high-yielding bond issues. On the other end of the spectrum, we have the stocks of large-cap established companies in defensive industries, like retail, agriculture, and health industries. Others include high-grade cash equivalents and investment bonds (bonds issued by corporations or the government for investment, not recurrent expenditure). Combining these two extremes gives a balanced portfolio that gives average returns with medium-level risk.

Portfolio Management
Creating an investment portfolio counts for nothing if it is poorly managed because then it does not fulfill its purpose of helping you achieve your investment objectives. Portfolio management entails the whole process of selecting a suitable investment policy. In its

most complex form, portfolio management is a finely tuned science that entails determining the best investment mix for you. This format of portfolio management is called active management, and it entails having an administrator who is constantly moving assets around with the intention to outmaneuver the market for the highest possible returns. Active management is best suited for short-term investments of up to seven years or in the last five or so years of a long investment period. The closer control reduces the risk of being caught flat-footed and minimizes risk.

At its simplest form, portfolio management entails simply the process of selecting the most suitable assets for the attainment of investment goals and bundling them together. This more relaxed method of managing an investment is known as passive management. The manager normally just observes the performance of assets and rarely interferes except when absolutely necessary. In passive management, there are no concerted efforts to outsmart the market. A passive style of portfolio management is best suited for long-term investments. The investor need not spend all their time poring over their portfolio; the due diligence analysis performed on the assets before inclusion in the portfolio is good enough to give one the peace of mind to simply sit back and watch.

Portfolio management comprises of three elements. The first one is the asset allocation described above. In asset allocation, the investor rigorously vets every stock, index, ETF, REIT, or whatever other assets they intend to invest in before committing to putting their money there. This ensures that no surprising new discoveries spring out later to mess up with the objectives for investing.

The second element of portfolio management is diversification. Diversification is necessitated by the fact that no one can possibly predict with accurate consistency the financial assets that are likely to give a good return and those that will flop. By combining assets from different classes, you can distribute the risk out so that when one asset generates a loss, another one posts a good gain and balances out the loss. We will discuss diversification in more detail below.

The third element of portfolio management is rebalancing, an exercise in realigning one's objectives with the contents of the portfolio. Rebalancing is done once every year in passive portfolio management and as often as possible in active management. While rebalancing, the investor considers gains made throughout the year and ensures that the balance of risky and conservative assets is maintained. For example, investors who decide on a 60/40 mix of high-risk to low-risk assets (because their risk tolerance requires such a mix) will do well to rebalance their portfolio before the higher gains made by the high-risk and high-return assets overpower the lower returns of low-risk assets and warp the balance of the portfolio in favor of high-risk assets. If the gains made by assets are not distributed in accordance with the original plan, the portfolio will soon be more aggressive than balanced.

Chapter 15 Tips and Tricks

Mastering the basics of investing is crucial for successful trading. However, there are a few more tips and tricks that beginners may try to improve their investing experience. There are several ways for investors to maximize their investments and get the greatest return possible. Investors may also consider using a 401k, 401b, or IRA to increase their returns. Investors may try a direct stock purchase plan. They may also try a dividend reinvestment plan. Finally, there are a few additional tips and tricks that may help investors to maximize their return and improve their investing experience as a whole.

Maximizing Your Investments

There are several ways that investors may maximize their investments. Of course, practicing proper trading techniques will help investors to earn greater returns on their investments. However, there are several other ways in which investors may maximize their investments and improve the returns on those investments. They may decrease investment costs, increase diversification, rebalance, and practice other techniques to improve their investments. It is important to learn about all the possible ways to maximize one's investments because you don't know what you don't know. Every bit counts. Just saving a bit here and there will quickly add up and maximize the investments.

Investors may maximize their investments by decreasing the cost of investing. There are several ways that investing may cost one money, and that money is coming directly out of the investment. Investors may switch from hiring a financial advisor to doing the investing themselves, cutting the costs of commission. Investors commonly forget about transaction costs. There is typically a flat fee for buying stock through a broker. Instead of making many small purchases, investors may save up and only buy stocks in certain increments (for example, perhaps the investor won't buy more stocks until they have saved $1000). By doing this, a much smaller percentage of the investment is being cut out and used to cover those fees. This may require more patience, but that money will add up. Lowering one's expenses will increase their return. Instead of being spent, that money may be growing and earning a return on it. Because of compound interest, this money will earn money on itself and multiply over a period of years. This is why it's crucial to save every bit possible.

Investors must also really pay attention to their portfolios. Diversification is crucial, and it can save the investor from losing all of their investment. Markets typically fall much more quickly than markets rise. This means that the investor must prepare for such occurrences. It is important to regularly rebalance one's portfolio to ensure that it is positioned correctly for the investor to make the largest possible gains.

Investors must also truly pay attention to what they want. Maximizing one's investments will depend on the person and what their goals are. Although it is wise to listen to the advice of experts and see what other ways that one may invest, it is crucial to follow the path that is best for the goals and preferences of the individual. This is why a plan is necessary and should be followed. Investors must not stop investing. This is another way to take advantage of compound interest. The investor's portfolio should never stop growing. This growth should be due to both growths in the investment and regular contributions by the investor themselves. Despite the great returns that may be experienced in a bull market, contributions are still necessary. Bear markets should also not discourage investors from continuing to invest; this can be a great time to get a good deal on a stock!

Retirement Plans

There are several savings plans that investors can get involved with. These can help to provide the investor with additional benefits that wouldn't be available to them otherwise.

One of these plans is a 401(k). This is a retirement savings plan that will be sponsored by an employer. This will allow the individual to invest their money before taxes so that they can save and invest some of their paychecks. The investor is not required to pay taxes until they withdraw this money from their account. Investors may control how to invest their money. It is common to have mutual funds that contain stocks, bonds, and money market investments. However, there are also target-date funds, which are stocks and bonds that will decrease in risk as the investor nears their retirement age. Unlike individual investing, however, this plan may not offer its users complete freedom. For instance, most employees must work for a company for a certain period of time before gaining access to their payments. Employees may even have to work for the company for a certain period of time before being able to enroll in a 401(k) at all. There are typical costs for withdrawing from these accounts before hitting retirement age as well. There are also contribution limits for each year. Investing for oneself, however, offers more freedom, and there are no limits on investing. For those working for an employer, however, this may be a good solution to investing using the paycheck given. It is a way to utilize the ability not to be taxed on one's investments from their paycheck. Employees may also enroll in Roth 401(k)s, which are not taxed for withdrawals. The better choice will depend on both the employee and the employer, as the plans are taxed differently.

403(b) plans are similar to 401(k)s, yet there are some slight differences. Both offer matching of the investments. For instance, for every dollar the employee contributes, the employer may contribute $0.50. This can prove to be greatly helpful to investors. The major difference between these are the employees that may enroll in these plans. Those in public schools, government jobs, nonprofits, and more may register for this plan. They are not for private-sector workers.

Besides this, the plans are identical in their purposes. A 403(b) plan, however, may allow for faster vesting of funds and additional contributions, although the investment options may be less plentiful.

There are also IRA plans. These are plans to save for retirement. These plans have different contribution limits, tax rules, and penalties for early withdrawals. Traditional IRAs are plans that are set up to save for retirement by the individual instead of by a company. The owner of the account will make contributions to the account. To open an account, the individual must have earned income during the year and be under 70.5 years of age. Simple IRAs are set up by small business owners for their employees. Both the owner of the account and their employee will contribute. To open an account, the employee must follow any rules set by their employer. Roth IRAs do not give a tax break when contributing, yet the retirement withdrawals are typically tax-free. Those wishing to enroll in such a plan should research their options. If given the option, the individual should research the pros and cons of their options and decide which will provide them with the best way to reach their goals. Some may not have the option given to them, yet it is wise to educate oneself on where their money is going. This may help to allow the individual to see more ways to maximize their investments.

Direct Stock Purchase Plans

Direct stock purchase plans allow investors to directly purchase stock from the company without the use of a broker. These plans may be available directly to retail investors, yet some companies will use third-party administrators to handle the transactions. They will typically have lower fees and the potential for buying shares at a discounted price. This may not be an option for all companies. These plans may also come with restrictions on when the investor may purchase shares. This plan may appeal to long-term investors that lack the money for an initial investment otherwise.

The investor may choose to sign up once for this plan, or they may sign up to make automatic and periodic investments through a transfer agent. This agent will maintain balances and record transactions. To keep costs low, transfer agents will typically carry out bulk transactions for the company each time period that they choose. Direct stock purchase plans are an alternative to using online brokerages, and they will typically cost less. Instead of paying higher transaction fees, the investor may pay a small purchase processing fee for each share that they purchase. These are usually quite a bit smaller than the transaction fees that investors must pay a brokerage. This means that the investor will have more money that they will be able to invest in. Instead of that money going to the brokerage, that money may be invested and generate a return for the investor. This can prove to be a wise move, especially for those wishing to buy a lesser amount of stocks. For those with greater funds for trading stocks, an online brokerage may prove more beneficial for the individual.

Direct stock purchase plans aren't for everyone. They will typically require investors to make a certain monthly commitment (i.e., $100) to investing. On the other hand, investors may buy stocks from a brokerage one time and never buy it again. Investors will also have to pay the market price for their stocks instead of being able to time it themselves. It may also be less convenient to create another account. However, once started, this will be an automatic investment and won't cost as much as it would purchase stocks through a broker.

This plan works by the investor making monthly deposits and those deposits being put towards purchasing shares of the company's stock. New shares (or portions of shares) will be purchased each month based on the amount of money available from deposits and dividends. This is a simple way to acquire shares of a company's stock slowly. This is also inexpensive, as these plans typically have either low costs or no costs at all. They also have low minimum deposits, usually ranging from about $100 to $500, although this may vary. This is a great plan for those who lack the financial power to invest otherwise. A common way that these purchase plans are carried out is by combining them with dividend reinvestment plans. These may be combined with the direct stock purchase plans to maximize the amount that the investor is investing in.

Dividend Reinvestment Plans

Dividend reinvestment plans allow investors to, as the name suggests, reinvest their dividends. These are typically free to sign up for and quite easy to get started in. Investors must simply check a box or click a few buttons to sign up, and the dividends that they earn will go towards reinvesting into shares of stocks. Perhaps the investor gets a dividend for stock x. If they have signed up for DRIP (Dividend Reinvestment Plan), that dividend will go towards shares (or portions of shares) of purchasing more of stock x. This is a great way to manage one's investments automatically. On the dividend payment date, the investor's dividend will go towards reinvesting in that stock.

There are ways to sign up for this through the brokerage that one trades through or through an investment company. Instead of taking out these dividends and spending them, they may be used for greater benefits to the investor. This money can help the investor to make more money. Instead of being received as a check or deposited into the investor's bank, this money may be redeposited into more stocks for the investor. The investor should keep in mind, however, that these shares will be bought at market price and will typically be bought directly from the company, which is why this is free of transaction costs. These shares will also not be marketable through stock exchanges; they must be redeemed through the company directly.

There may be some limitations to this. Although these may be commission-free for the investor and may even have discounted share prices, DRIPs may have minimum dollar amounts that must be invested. There may be a minimum purchase amount for this. This is a great way for investors to take advantage of compound interest, as they are adding the extra amount that they may not have invested otherwise. However, the dividends may still be taxable, and the shares will be illiquid. The investor, once they have signed up, will not be able to regulate how much is and is not reinvested from these dividends. It is also a great way for investors to increase the number of shares of stock that they own without paying a commission for these shares. This is a more cost-effective approach than buying stock traditionally.

Other Tips and Tricks

There are several tips and tricks that investors swear by. These may be used to the investor's advantage, or they may be ignored. The most important tip to remember when investing is to stick to one's individual goals. Despite countless advice available to investors, the best plans and actions come from the investor themselves. After all, every investor has their own personal preferences when it comes to stocks. Some wish to invest for the long-term and choose low-risk investment options while others risk more and invest for a shorter term. The investor themselves has the greatest say on what is best for them.

Some investors prefer to invest in index funds instead of investing in multiple stocks. This can decrease risk, increase diversification, and take less time to research and manage than otherwise investing in individual stocks. Investors may also consider mutual funds to lower their risk even more. These will provide investors with lower risk and higher returns. It will also help the investor to maintain a diversified portfolio. The investor may automate their investments to do so by choosing Robo-advisors or other like investment tools.

Investors must balance patience and commitment. Although it may seem wise to time the market, investors must continue to contribute during all times. There may be times, however, where the investor must practice patience to ensure that they are choosing transactions that have the best timing. The stock market is constantly changing. Above all, the investor must stick to the goals that they set prior to investing. The investor must always consider the long-term effects of their actions. While it may be tempting to respond quickly to emotional or instinctual feelings, the long-term is what must be invested. Investors must not let emotions take over their investments. It is important not to let fear control when the investor sells their stocks and not to let greed determine when to buy stocks. The investor should stick to their plan carefully. This plan should have been made prior to investing to ensure that the investor is following a logical plan that is not influenced by emotions or instincts.

Diversification is important. It is important to not only diversify the sectors and stocks that one invests in but also to diversify the amount of risk that each stock will be to the investor. This means that the investor is opening themselves up to higher returns yet still maintaining a certain level of security when it comes to investing. It is important to diversify among different classes and sectors, though. Certain industries may take a hit at once, which is why the investor should diversify their investments.

Chapter 16 What is the stock market?

Trading times on the stock exchange

Maybe you do not know it, but trading on the stock exchange offers the possibility of dealing online continuously or 24 hours a day, thanks to the overlapping of the opening hours of the different international stock markets. In fact, the world's big financial centers are eight and their trading hours are listed in three major sessions: the Asian session, the European session and the North American session.

But we must also take into account the legal and solar hours that are not the same depending on the time zone. Let's take a look at the most influential time zones for the stock market.

The Asian session

At the beginning of the week the Asian session is the first one to open. This session includes the stock exchange centers of Japan, China, Australia, New Zealand and Russia as well as other smaller centers. Asian assets and currency pairs including currencies of these countries are therefore the most volatile in these times. The same applies to economic publications.

The trading hours of the Asian session are as follows:

Opening hours of the Asian market: at 4 in summer and 3 in winter

Closing time of the Asian market: at 8 in summer and 7 in winter

The European session:

The European session is obviously the most interesting for European investors. It is the second to open after the Asian session and also regroups several major stock exchanges including Italy, France, Germany, Switzerland or the United Kingdom. It should be noted that London's financial center is the largest in the world and more than 30% of financial transactions are carried out in this center every day. Trading volumes are therefore very high during the European session and therefore involve extremely volatile and interesting movements in terms of trading.

The trading hours of the European session are as follows:

European market opening hours: 12.00 in the summer and 12.00 in the winter

Closing time of the European market: at 16 in summer and at 17 in winter

The North American session:

Finally comes the North American session, which is therefore the last to open and close the market cycle. Obviously, this session is also one of the most followed by traders all over the world because it is during this period that US assets are traded. This session includes the financial markets of the United States but also of Canada, Mexico and the countries of South America. It is on the stock market in New York that the volatility is higher at this time of day.

The trading hours of the North American session are as follows:

Opening time of the North American market: at 17 in summer and at 17 in winter

Closing time of the North American market: at 21 in summer and at 22 in winter

History and general knowledge

The Stock Exchange is the market where sellers and buyers can trade values, foreign currencies, services and goods. The stock exchange thus becomes an important place to put companies in touch, looking for resources to support their production, and investors.

Already in the Middle Ages, the scholarship gathered merchants and notaries who dedicated themselves to mercantile and financial activities.

In the twelfth century, Venice became the main Italian square; here were introduced some innovations later adopted by other cities such as the negotiation of the public debt and the turn of the bill.

Bruges, in West Flanders, is the first European city to have a physical place for exchange, where the sale takes place according to new stock exchange rules. The industrial revolution leads to the birth of modern bags in Italy, following the example of Bruges (Trieste, Rome, Milan, Florence, Naples, Turin, Genoa, Bologna, Palermo and Venice).

We can distinguish two types of market based on the services and products exchanged:

1. the stock exchange;
2. the goods exchange.

The Stock Exchange is the market in which financial instruments already in circulation are exchanged, such as bonds, shares, futures, warrants, etc.; as a consequence, the stock exchange is a secondary market (in the primary markets, investors buy the goods as soon as they reach the market).

In the goods exchange, the sale involves goods of different types, placed in appropriate warehouses. Here buyers and sellers can exchange the deposit policies, which guarantee the presence of the goods and the right of withdrawal.

The sale and purchase of outstanding securities is regulated by precise rules; once the system of the on-call auction was over, where the agents exchanged paper documents, the market takes place via an electronic circuit where it is also possible to exchange government bonds and bonds.

Among the main types of shares we distinguish the ordinary ones, as they assign precise administrative and financial rights to the holder (right to vote in the meetings, to request assembly, liquidation, option, etc.).

Preferred stock (preferred shares) guarantee special property rights to the owners; in the event of dissolution of the company, for example, "privileges" are granted in the distribution of profits (as provided for in the company by-laws).

Savings shares grant ownership rights to assets; however they exclude administrative rights, including the right to vote.

Poster-gate shares provide for limitations in both administrative and patrimonial rights (generally excluding voting rights).

Limited-voting shares include special restrictions on administrative rights, such as voting limited to certain topics; according to the Italian law, they must guarantee property privileges to the owner.

As previously mentioned, the financial market is structured in financial centers, where various financial services are treated.

The largest financial center is New York, where the Nyse is located (the New York Stock Exchange all commodities), the Nasdaq (technology stocks) and the Amex (the American Stock Exchange collects many small capitalization companies that sell securities of various kinds).

Other important financial centers include Tokyo and London (the most important in Europe).

The Milan Stock Exchange, also known as Piazza Affari, controls the main Italian markets and plays a very relevant role.

Chapter 17 Terms that it is important to know

Before getting started, it is important to learn the basic terms and how they are used by the experts. In this chapter, you will find a simplified dictionary with the most popular words related to the investing niche.

Stock market

The stock market is the digital place where the largest number of transactions involving the shares, ie the shares of corporate capital, takes place.

In Italy, for example, the stock market is called MTA - Electronic Stock Market - and it should be noted that it does not coincide with the famous "Borsa di Piazza Affari", but represents one of the most important segments.

In fact, at Piazza Affari, different types of financial instruments are traded and the market is divided according to the type of contracts traded in:

- MTA, the electronic stock market;
- SEDEX, the segment in which instruments such as covered warrants and certificates are traded;
- MOT, the electronic bond market in which bonds like (with the exception of those

convertible into shares), government bonds, Eurobonds and ABS, ie securities deriving from the security of loans are traded;
- TAH, After hours, the electronic market in which it is possible to negotiate after the closing of the Exchange, but only for the instruments of the MTA (shares) and the SEDEX (covered warrants and certificates);
- ETF plus, the electronic market in which UCITS units or shares are traded (SGRs and Sicavs);
- IDEM, the market for derivative instruments (futures and option contracts on currencies, interest rates and financial instruments). Exceptions are forwarders that are derivative contracts traded on OTC markets, over the counter, that is not regulated.

Market capitalization

The stock market is also divided into sections by capitalization threshold.

What, however, is the market capitalization?

The size of a listed company is measured in capitalization, that is, the value given by the number of shares available for that company multiplied by their market price.

The sections in which common markets are divided are:

- Blue chip, where the shares of the 40 largest companies are traded (over 1000 million euros);
- Mid Cap, where the securities of the 60 listed companies with high capitalization are traded but which do not fall among the Blue chips;
- Small Cap, where the shares of companies that do not fall between the Blue chips or the Mid Cap are bought or sold;
- Micro Cap, for companies that do not fall within the minimum liquidity criteria necessary for the other segments;
- Star, for companies with a capitalization of between 40 and 1,000 million euro, but with high transparency, governance and liquidity requirements;
- MTA International where the shares of companies listed on EU exchanges are traded.

Stocks

The stocks are portions in the shared capital of companies, incorporated in joint-stock companies. The two main types of stocks are:

- Ordinary Stocks, are those held by the shareholders of a company. They hold voting rights in corporate assemblies and profits deriving from dividends and capital gains;

- Savings Stocks, shares of this type do not have voting rights, but they guarantee patrimonial privileges such as dividends, ie the distribution of profits. They are mainly intended for small investors.

Stock value

Each share of each company is traded or bought or sold on a price basis: the market value. This price evolves continuously on the basis of the number and the sign of the contracts concluded.

For example, if you read that the Enel stock is up today, it means that many investors are buying Enel shares.

For the classical laws of economic demand and supply, if the demand rises, the price also rises. At the end of the day, when the session is officially closed, the official price of the Enel share will be obtained in this case, by the result of all the fluctuations that the value of the stock suffered during the session based on the number of exchanges it is traded on.

What drives an investor to buy the shares of a company at that particular moment? As we have already said, the formation of share prices is a dynamic process like any other commodity market.

The value of a company stock affects:

- corporate performance (the state of health of the company, the size of its assets, future growth prospects, ownership structures, extraordinary finance transactions such as

acquisitions, mergers and demergers): the improvement in performance is matched by an increase in price and investor's propensity to buy those shares; vice versa, the opposite happens, that is, depreciation. Who owns those shares will sell them, increase the bid and drop the price in question;
- performance of the sector, or the performance at the same time of other companies belonging to the same sector, also on other global stock exchanges;
- macro or foreign policy data directly or indirectly relevant to a company: positive news generate purchases and appreciation, negative news push sales and the depreciation of the stock;
- news or rumors about the company, such as the discovery of new deposits for companies in the oil sector, or the registration of a new patent for a company in the pharmaceutical sector or news about possible mergers, joint ventures or acquisitions.

CFD

This is a key point that actually explains why there is much less bureaucracy for forex trading than for buying and selling bank shares. CFDs (Contract for Difference) are contracts for differences that follow the performance of a given underlying (share, currency, index, etc.) and that can be exchanged, that is, bought or sold. CFDs differ from shares because they are not co-owned by a company and therefore do not give voting rights to those holding them. However, CFDs offer the same economic benefits as equities, such as profits, dividends and splits.

In even more technical terms, the CFD exchanges the difference in value between the opening price of a certain underlying security (eg share) and its closing price. Following this mechanism, the trader who negotiates CFDs:

1. Gets a positive result if it buys before the underlying goes up
2. Gets a negative result if it sells before the underlying goes down

The mechanism is very simple and we are sure that it is already clear. We need to buy if we think that a stock is close to the upside, we need to sell it if we think that a stock is close to the downside. CFDs follow the values of the underlying assets, so you can get positive results just like shareholders, but playing at home from the comfort of your home.

Chapter 18 Master The Mystic Arts

In this segment, we will concern ourselves with the issue of timing. I mean, from the earlier portion about identification of potential home run stocks, we will have to choose a time on when we need to take a stand with those chosen stocks. Figuring out the intrinsic value will not do us any good if we do not simply get our skin in the game.

This portion is all about letting us know when should be the windows of optimal timing with which to place our stake and watch the drama unfold. I am not talking about placing your trades during the times when the moonlight shines the brightest or during the winter solstice or summer equinox. That is not what I mean when we are talking about windows of optimal timing. There are schools of thought which believe in such trading methodology but I have yet to meet a truly consistently successful performer who employs such arts.

The window of opportunity that will present itself to us actually boils down to the movement of price. The price of the chosen stock, which we have sieved through countless hundreds via our fundamental analysis.

Why is this guy talking about price, what does he actually mean? Those could be the questions running through your head right now and you are absolutely right to have them. The answers all lie with technical analysis of the stock market.

Technical Analysis And How To Train For It

Before you go all excited and eager to learn and unleash this supposed holy grail instrument of mass destruction for the stock market, think again. I have always said there is no such thing as a holy grail. Ditto for technical analysis.

To recap again, technical analysis is the study of the movements and fluctuations of the price as well as volume numbers of the chosen stock or counter. This is because it is believed that the price is the honest ultimate reflection of what the market thinks about the stock. It is the culmination of all the insider trading, the institutional investing, the retail and large scale trading that finally aggregates itself into a single price for that particular time period. As the price moves, technical analysts track how it moves and then make forecasts or decisions based on those movements.

As I have said before, the schools of technical analysis are far and wide, with many utilizing technical signaling devices in order to make their call. I personally do not practice those ways because I have tried them before and found that this kind delayed signaling does not really work for me.

Think about it, a moving average is in essence the average of the prices over a stated period of time, the longer the period of average, the smoother and less reactive it would be to the actual price. This is a common theme running through most of the technical indicators we have today in all markets. They are all derivatives of price and hence would then tend to be somewhat laggy as compared to actual price movement. Consequently, their powers of prediction are also somewhat off.

For me, I personally like to work with the actual price itself. It is cleaner, and actually a whole lot simpler to process. You do not have to concern yourself with all the different parameters of the technical indicator, nor do you have to worry about changing those said parameters in order to suit a particular trading period or style.

Many folks however, treat price action as some sort of mystic art. I, too had those thoughts when I was enamored with finding the perfect parameter for my stochastics and Relative Strength Index indicator. I have come to realize, the reason why technical indicators are still popular and widely used today is because it is somewhat like the elementary school. It is easy to grasp, and definitely easy to use. Anyone with just a little familiarization practice could just set it up and start investing immediately based off the signals. There is also the hype as well of course, where many folks have come out in the open and touted the superiority of their technical systems. Some claims would entail working only for one hour a day and getting passive income to replace your day job. Others would go for the big ticket and claim millionaire status within six or even three months.

Sadly, there will always be folks who fall for these claims.

It represents money without having to put in too much effort, while it also retains the believability because you are actually still involved. You are the one to set the system up, wait for the signal and then decide on triggering the trade based on the signal. Many people, like me at first, would baulk at learning price action technical analysis because it just seems so wide and vast, and there was no structure or system to babysit us.

I would like to tell you this to be not exactly true. There is a structure of sorts, and you definitely will be able to learn price action if you honestly put in the effort. Let's talk about what kind of efforts you would need to put in.

Candlesticks

Japanese candlesticks may seem daunting, with their many myriad combinations. Patterns that involve a single candlestick, three, five and even seven sticks! All these could sound potentially mind boggling but there is some good news on the horizon.

You may go ahead and master all the Japanese candlestick patterns, it will be your express choice and it is purely an option. You do not need to master all patterns. I will repeat this. You do not need to master all patterns.

For me, I am more concerned with single candlestick signals and what they tend to present in terms of bull or bear indications.

Two of the most commonly searched for candlesticks in my book would be the toppish or bearish shooting star.

It looks like an inverted t. It is usual that the body of the candle is shorter than that of the wick or the shadow or tail. Multiple names but all mean the part that is pointing upward. The reason why there is a long tail is that there was an upward movement during the time period. Take the example of a day shooting star candle. During the day, there was bullish intent and the price was pushed up, however, whether it was just a fake flush by the stop hunters or a real push by the bulls which ended up failing, the bears took over and pushed the price back down. This creates the longish tail.

With a shooting star, this represents bearish intent for the coming periods and we will thus prepare ourselves for it. The usual way of how we search for such candlesticks would be near resistance price levels and bands. If there were to be quite a number clustered together, it would tell a story that the bulls attempted to push through that price level but failed and hence ceding control over to the bears. When spotted, our natural intent would be to short that particular counter.

The other common candlestick pattern would be of the bullish intent, which is commonly known as the hammer. Why? It literally looks like one when presented in the candlestick format. It is quite the opposite of the shooting star, with the long tail pointing downward instead of upwards.

As you might have guessed, bears tried to push the price down, failed in that attempt during that specific period, and the bulls charged the price back up again. This is usually a bullish candle.

At this point in time, I would like to take the chance to state quite categorically that you do not have to be too anal with analyzing candlestick patterns. What I mean is, as long as the candle approximates to a shooting star or a hammer, then acknowledge it as such. There is absolutely no need to examine every small detail of the candlestick and try to fit it into the various different candlestick patterns on the textbook. There is no need to be over thinking when it comes to candlestick patterns.

When I see rough approximations to hammers or shooting stars, I accept them as it is and just add their signal into my overall aggregation of the decision for that particular counter.

There is also another candlestick pattern which I think is fairly important and that is called the doji. The doji looks like this.

+

A literal plus sign. This is a sign that the market is undecided and the bears and bulls have no power over each other. The usual stance when we see a doji would be to adopt a wait and see approach.

For me though, I like to think that every price chart is trying to tell a story, and a doji appearing at a crucial point may tell of something more significant than just simple indecision. Think about this, you have a stock that has been on the downward trend for some periods, and then a doji appears at a substantive price level. This tells us that there definitely is a pause in the downward momentum of the counter, but as to what the stock may do next would then depend on your knowledge of the strength of that price level.

A similar situation happening in a space that has no significant price levels would probably mean that the bears are just really taking a breather, and will continue the slaughter after having their rest.

This is how we start to piece and surmise things from the clues which the market provides us.

This is also the reason why I am of mind that you do not really have to know all the candlestick patterns. There is no need to create more potential confusion for yourself. To be honest, when I teach my folks, I just tell them to pay attention to the shooting star, the doji and the hammer.

That's it.

The shooting star and hammer represent the extremes and also the exhaustion of the prior trend, and hence it has quite a bit of power in foretelling a reversal in the direction of price, especially when the candle happens on a day, month or even a yearly candle. Remember, larger the time period, the stronger the signal.

The doji as I mentioned earlier, would be either indecision or a resting point, and that usually you have got to pair it with support and resistance bands in order to get better clarity on its true nature.

Having said all the above, I would also like to point out that candlestick patterns are meant to help and provide more clues for you to piece together a coherent, workable story regarding the stock in question. You are not going to pull the trigger based on the occurrence of a pattern.

Some course on price action do teach triggers via candlestick patterns, but for me, I don't practice it as such. Clues they are, and clues they shall remain. I prefer to have more information on hand before making any potential moves which involves my cash to be honest!

Periods

We have touched on this topic before in an earlier section but I would like to speak about this again with respect to its importance in the field of technical analysis. Periods are what we refer to as time periods. It can be as short as one minute, to an hour long, or as lengthy as a day or a month. This means that an entire candle is encapsulated in one month if we were looking at a monthly candlestick.

The longer the period, the more conviction and staying power it has for that candle, and hence the more valuable its accompanying signal will be. A trigger on a one minute candle would be much weaker when held against a trigger on a day candle. By this, we can simply think that it is much easier to trust the day candle versus the one minute candle. In a similar vein, it will be much easier to trust a month candle when it is held up against a day candle.

When we analyze charts, it is always good practice to zoom out straight to the largest time frame possible. For me, that usually means going straight to the month chart or even the yearly chart, where one candlestick represents one month or one year. This way of looking at things ensures that you have quite the macro view at the very start, which is always a good place to initiate your chart investigation. You want to use the clues on the chart to piece together a coherent story which will then help to structure an execution plan for the investment target.

Going in from the big time frames will also ensure that you will have the best opportunity to take a look at the history of the price movement. The up and downtrends of the stock should be evident, as well as potential sideways movement. Of course, our final object of interest will always be the movement area that is closest to the most recently presented candle on the chart itself. We want to see if it is an upward, downward or just a sideways kind of trend.

The beauty of a larger time frame chart is that these trends become much clearer as compared to when it is viewed on a lower timeframe. The old adage of trading with the trend holds some weight, and that is the reason why we would want to know what the stock is doing on the higher timeframe.

For many folks who are just starting out, or who may be already having some experience with charting, one of the most common issues would be the conflict between the lower and higher timeframes. What do I mean by this?

Imagine you have a chart which you are looking at it on the day period and it is telling you that it is a period of sideways movement. You want to double check on the higher time frame and see if there is coherence and you switch to the weekly chart. On the weekly chart you do see some evidence of sideways movement but you think that you need more confirmation because what you see does not seem to convince you thoroughly.

You then move up to the monthly chart. When looking through the lens of a month chart, you see that the stock is in fact trending downwards. You then merge these two findings together and formulate a plan. A day sideways movement, coupled with a month downward trend would probably mean that you would have a higher probable win rate if you were to do short selling when the stock nears any resistance levels and to take quicker profit when it nears the support bands. The short selling is in line with the monthly downward trend, whilst the selling on the high and taking faster profit on the support level conforms to the day sideways trend.

This is also applicable when you are doing day trading. It is just that we zoom down to lower time frames. Usually we would look at the day chart to get a gist of how the overall trend is going to be like, then we would push further down into the hourly chart and then further down into the fifteen minute chart or the five minute chart for the actual triggering.

The principles are always the same, we want to move in accordance as much as possible with the higher time frame because that is what will give us more confidence. We can then utilize the lower time frames to pull our triggers for trade initiation.

Another thing I want to point out would be the trade-off. In situations where we wait to initiate or confirm trades on the higher time frame, that would also usually mean we would probably get in at a less advantageous price when compared to pulling the trigger on the signal from the lower time frame.

More confirmation would mean taking more time, which also means bearing the risk of having a lousier price to trigger your trade on. Going in on the lower time frames would mean quicker speed and in most cases better price in terms of trade execution, but it means bearing the risk that it could just be a fake signal and having the trade go south on you.

For me, I always would tend toward more confirmation, because I have had the experience of doing too many lower timeframe trades and I just did not really enjoy the taste of it.

I mean, automation is great these days, but for most retail players, we would still retain quite a bit of manual control on the trades. Triggering one trade based on the day chart sounds better to me versus fifteen trades based on the five minute chart. Of course, it goes back to your trading psyche as well. So if you are the adrenaline junkie kind, well, perhaps you might really get to enjoy punching in trades every five minutes, who knows!

What about getting in on the less favorable price you say? That is the reason why we call it the trade-off. More confirmation and you pay more in terms of the entry price. It is just like a concert where you have to pay more in order to be closer to the stage, where you can observe the action much closer and better.

Personally, there is part of my trading persona where I know that I am pretty cool if I don't get the trade, because I can simply wait for the next better one. I know for certain there will always be a next one coming, in part because of my trust in my system, and also because I have been seeing it work for that many years. With this little facet of my trading psychology, I then devise a workaround with regards to the less favorable price upon higher timeframe confirmation.

When I first see the trigger on the higher timeframe, I will not execute a market order. This means I do not just jump in at the price which is the current market price. I will take a look at the nearest, logical support or resistance level and then park a limit order which will usually get me a better price as compared to the market price.

This means I do not get the luxury of having exposure in the trade call by doing the market order, but instead I choose to trade that luxury for a better price entry and it is somewhat of a side bet that I judge the price would retrace back to my limit orders.

This also means that on some occasions, I will have to totally forgo the trade altogether because the price just does not retrace back to any of my limit orders. In the case of a bullish trade, the stock price just zooms straight up with nary a look backwards, and I can just wave forlornly goodbye in the distance. I mean I used to, not anymore these days.

This method is pretty much a double or nothing mentality, which I personally use to circumvent the issue of having to pay too much in order to initiate a trade or investment.

It can also be pretty trying at times, because you could have set your limit buy orders for example, and the stock price moves up, and it could be days or weeks even, before it finally decides to come back down and touch your limits. During that interim period, you might be emotionally roller-coaster, so it might be a good idea to really get a grip on your trading psychology and emotions first before deciding if this method is one which you might be tempted to try.

Of course, when it works, you get the satisfaction of having the right trade, with the added conviction of the higher timeframe signal, as well as a pretty good price to boot. This would also mean more profit margins for you due to the larger differential between the entry and target profit price.

When it doesn't work, I just dust it off and carry on to the next trade. You cannot win all of them, and the danger in trying to do so far outstrips any potential rewards it may offer.

So for this topic of timeframe, it is most important that I impress upon you the value of the higher timeframe chart. You can start by zooming straight to the higher timeframe whenever you are analyzing any stock chart, as this will put your mind in a macro frame so you will be seeing the bigger picture.

During my earlier trainings, I used to flip through countless higher timeframe charts of different companies, and observe how companies in the same industries might have similar chart movements, while others may have their differences as well. For those with the same movements, you would also notice the movement direction may be the same for the similar time period, but the degree of movement would have their nuanced differences.

Another interesting facet would be spotting a company in the same industry that has different chart movement from all its major competitors, and that would be a clue worthy of further investigation. Some of the hidden gems might be just hiding in plain sight for all we know, and it just needs a little more probing to let it see the light.

There is no running away from effort and work when it comes to all forms of stock and investment analysis. I guess that is the ultimate message which I would like to send across to you or anyone reading this. Stock chart reading is a skill, just like riding a bicycle or fishing. It can be learnt and picked up, further ruminated upon and polished into an art form.

This is the reason why some folks may just take a glance at a price chart and know in an instant if there is any opportunity or not. They have majored this form of analysis into a skill that is close to an art form, and at times, they may find it hard to explain their decisions to others. This was what happened to me when I was first apprenticing under one of my mentors. He was someone so ingrained in the market that it seemed he was operating on feeling and intuition. His most common phrase to me during my tutelage was "it's very simple, as plain as day".

Of course, I struggled with that every single time he uttered those words. I simply could not see what he was seeing and it was really some time and effort later which then let me discover my stock charting eyes.

So, take heart if it looks all mumbo jumbo to you at the present, because there really is a light at the end of the tunnel, and it is honestly a question of you finishing that walk down the tunnel and emerging well into the sunshine. It can be done. Just stick to the principles and stay hungry to better yourself. You will be fine.

Alright, that was a slight pep talk, so back to the other aspects of technical analysis which I find important.

Wave Theory

Some of you may have heard of the intriguing theory called Elliot Wave theory. The long and short of it is these waves are supposed to be extremely predictive in nature, and that means if you manage to master reading Elliot waves, you are thus able to trade and invest with ease.

Generally, in an uptrend, you should have five waves, and then when it comes to a retracement, there should be three waves. This makes for a total of eight waves for an up movement, with its accompanying draw down. The same goes for a downtrend. The downward portion will have five waves while its retracement will also be spotted as having three waves.

Sounds good right?

One big nefarious issue here is this. There seems to be no logical base for getting started with your wave one. That means any place can be deemed as the start of wave one, and you can imagine the messy disputes when various Elliot wave technicians meet each other.

The other big issue with wave theory is that it is very much a fractal concept. This means, in a major up wave one, you will also have within that single one wave, a whole set of five waves up and three waves down.

And this can literally keep on going down to the smaller time periods.

As one who has tried his hand in pure Elliot wave counting, I can assure you that I have not really mastered it. There simply seems to be so many different starting points and I have absolutely no idea as to which wave should belong to which.

Maybe others have had better results with it, but so far I have not really seen anyone doing that well with just pure Elliot wave counting.

Why are we then talking about waves, if there seem to be so many diverse issues surrounding its proper usage?

The key reason is this, we need a basic understanding of waves in order to help us with the chart reading.

You can ignore the portions about wave counting and all its associated burdens, but the crux that you have to catch would be the actual visual recognition of a wave when presented to you on the candlestick chart. The whole purpose of getting to know Elliot wave is simply to let us get more acquainted with the visual aspects of seeing and recognizing the up and down waves as shown via the price movements.

On one hand, I see some folks heaving a sigh of relief that they do not have to step into that confusing mire that is actual Elliot wave counting, while on the other hand, I also see some people questioning if this is it? The whole purpose of knowing wave theory is just so that you get a better visual yardstick with which you use for charting.

The simple answer is yes. It really is for that purpose. To be frank, some people actually try to automate this wave charting process, but I find that the analysis produced to be of a distinct inferior vintage as compared to the manual, visual process.

One of the things which actually help with wave recognition is the definition of an up and down trend.

For an uptrend, you should be seeing higher price points than its previous high, while seeing higher lows as compared to its previous lows. The crux of the uptrend is always its higher lows. An uptrend which is obvious will have higher highs to complement those higher lows, but it can also have stagnant highs as well. This means we see a kind of flat plateau of price highs, with its accompanying higher price lows. This also qualifies as an uptrend too.

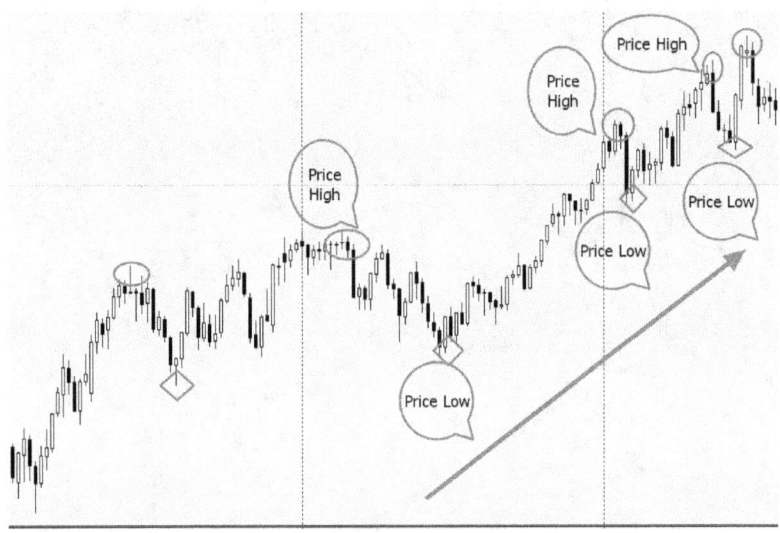

For the downtrend, the reverse will be true. Lower price highs will be the key here as well, while lower price lows will be present in a straight forward downtrend. It is essentially the uptrend in reverse. In order to verify that a downtrend is indeed happening on a stock or counter, we want to spot its lower highs. In the event that the price lows are all staying flat without putting up a show of reaching for lower lows, it still qualifies as a downtrend as long as the lower highs are in place. What happens if we see a situation where there are lower highs, and yet the stock also displays higher lows? This then becomes a strike out from the downtrend definition, and you would not be advised to classify the price movement as that of a downward trend any longer.

The same situation goes for the uptrend. Should you observe higher lows, while there is also a formation of lower highs ongoing, then the classification of upward trend should no longer be labelled onto that particular stock.

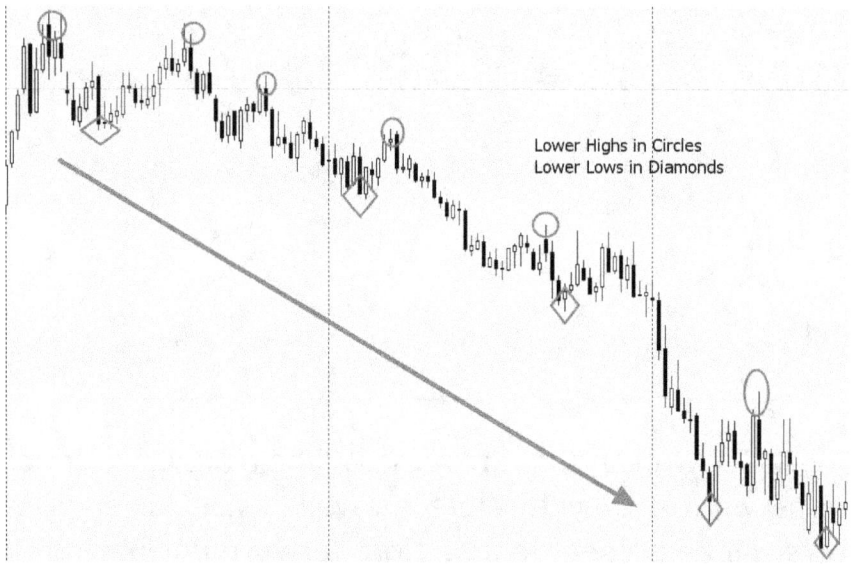

Lower Highs in Circles
Lower Lows in Diamonds

When you have the concepts of up and downtrend firmly in place, you would be in a much better place to recognize the price movements when they form in relation to the candlesticks.

There might be an inclination to overanalyze initially, especially when it comes to folks who are beginners. It is wholly normal to do that, but it is definitely not encouraged. I would have to say the overzealous analysis would somehow pave the way for faster and more accurate recognition of the waves within the price movements.

For me, I literally looked at charts for hours on end, and coupled that with actual live trading as well so that each trade becomes a teacher on its own. When folks practice stock market investing and charting in this manner, the experiential process is much stronger and you actually might learn faster.

I will come right out and say as I always do, that there is no immediate shortcut to success with regards to this. I have seen some folks pick it up very quickly, like in a few short months they are able to grasp the finer details and concepts and more importantly utilize it firmly for their own charting purposes. There are others who are a tad slower, and their learning process may take upwards of a year or so.

Regardless of which it may be for yourself, it would be wise to note that everyone's learning process will be different, and slow or fast does not necessarily mean for the better. I can be numbered amongst those that needed a year or so in order to truly see the price movements for what they were, and I would say it did me no great harm putting in those extra hours because it served to deepen my knowledge on the workings of the stock market.

When we examine price waves, and delve further into the trends, we will invariably encounter chart patterns along the way. I shall not be touching too much into this topic at this juncture, because I believe them to be more suitable for a book that is dedicated more toward the technical analysis side of things. We can however, touch a little before we move on to the next major topic.

Remember the example I gave about the up and downtrends? Recall also the part where I mentioned for the case of an uptrend, and you start seeing higher lows as well as lower highs? That is in fact an example of a chart pattern called the symmetric triangle.

For the case when you have higher lows but encounter a plateau of similar highs, this will also be a chart pattern called the ascending triangle.

For the reverse situation where you see lower highs and same lows, this will be a chart pattern called descending triangle.

Though all are triangles, you do not treat them the same way. The central theme to triangles is that traditional investing and trading lore would say that these patterns indicate a compression of impetus and momentum, hence triangles always represent price break outs. We should expect to see strong movements in price when these patterns eventually bear fruit.

The way to trade them, however, is not the same.

For ascending and descending triangles, because we can still label them as being up or downtrends, the expectation would be for prices to continue on in their previous direction. An ascending triangle would see price break up, while a descending triangle would see price break down.

For the symmetric triangle, this is a bit trickier because the price can move either way. It can turn out to be what the folks call a continuation pattern, in which the price continues on its previous trajectory, or it may evolve to become a reversal pattern. In this case, the price will execute a sharp reverse of its previous heading. Up becomes down and down become up.

The traditional way of trading these triangles mostly involves trading on the breakout. This means you wait for the price candle to close above the line that you draw when you trace the shape of the triangle using its corresponding candlesticks. Some will advocate waiting for three candlesticks after the initial break. This all depends on the time frame which you are looking at to be honest. If you are already on the day candlestick, I would reckon that one single candle close would be more than sufficient to guard yourself against an instance of a fake price breakout. For folks on the lower time frame, then perhaps waiting for one or three more candlesticks would be somewhat prudent.

Again, there is the trade-off present here again. The more confirmation you want, the higher probability you have got to pay a higher entry price. In the days when I was trading breakouts without the use of price levels, I circumvented this issue by parking the limit orders again.

Yes, those limit orders again.

I have got to say they are pretty useful, and the benefits of using them more than outweigh the cost of missing out the trade in my opinion.

These days, I do not just jump into a trade whenever I see triangles. It is always good to pair chart patterns with the corresponding support and resistance levels in order to derive a better probability winning trade.

This is also what I would term as the danger contained within the usage of chart patterns for execution purposes. Once you start looking for patterns, you can literally see them anywhere, on any time frame. Try it! You won't be disappointed and can almost always spot any chart pattern.

This will present an ever-present temptation to trade each and every chart pattern, and that is not what I would recommend. I did that before, and it was both exhausting as well as not rewarding. Chart patterns have a lot more significance when they are forming or formed on significant price levels, and it would be good to use chart patterns as yet another clue for the analysis of a potential trade or investment idea.

These days, I don't execute based on chart patterns alone. They serve me more as confirmatory as well as early warning signals for any stocks that I might be monitoring. Having a chart pattern form on any of your filtered stocks should be good news, either to warn against entry for now, or to support the decision to take exposure.

To sum up this segment, looking at how the price move and formulating an understanding of it within the structure of waves, up and downtrend movements would be crucial to develop further understanding for stock market analysis. With this analysis, it would then create a much better informed environment in order to make buy and sell calls.

Stock market investment does not always remain difficult. It is a subject that rewards people who constantly put in effort to understand and learn. In time, analysis becomes much quicker and more accurate, while the win ratio for your trade and investment calls will see an uptick. Also, when you trade better, your understanding of your personal trading psychology will also naturally blossom. This will stand you in good stead in daily life as well, because you will possess an awareness of your personal mental and emotional triggers, which may allow you to steer clear of potential future pitfalls.

Screening for Stocks that Satisfy Our Portfolio Requirements

At this point, you might be asking yourself, "How do I know which stocks to analyze," "where do I even begin," or "what am I supposed to do with all of these wealth-building portfolio rules?" Not to worry –the wonderful world of online stock screeners has our backs! As the name implies, stock screeners are software tools, usually Internet based, that allow investors to search or "screen" for investments based on pre-determined criteria, often referred to as "filters." As such, stock screeners narrow the investment universe from thousands of stocks, mutual funds, ETFs, etc. to a select few that meet investors' needs. share price of $15 or higher, etc.), and the fundamental requirements discussed in this chapter (e.g. PEG ratio of "1" or less, etc.). With the right stock screener, we can simply plug in the values of our requirements (a few more rules will be added in later chapters) and out pops a list of stocks screened to meet our defined criteria.

In addition, there are many free online stock screeners that can be found around on the Internet. The sophistication and usefulness of these screeners vary depending on investor needs. Populate the fields with the appropriate rule values, and the screen will automatically update as parameters are added.

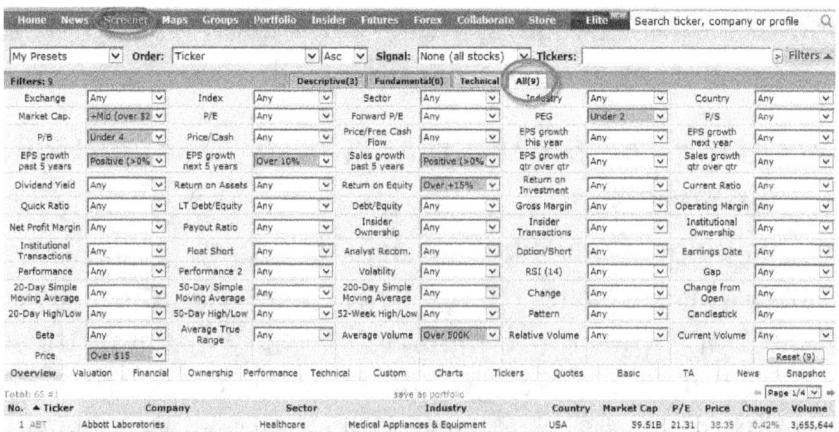

Chapter 19 Tools for Profitable Trading

In this chapter, we will be looking at the tools you can use in order to make sound investment decisions.

To make sound decisions, you need to base them on solid fundamentals. That is why the tools presented in this chapter are financial models which can help you evaluate the performance of a company.

Upon proper evaluation, you can determine if the stock is right for you, or you can take a pass on it until its fundamentals improve.

As such, we will be discussing five models which you can put into practice right away.

These models are based on quantitative analysis. Much like technical analysis, quantitative analysis refers to basing decisions on the number and measurable data.

While your instincts are definitely important, it is data-driven analytics that will give you the peace of mind that you need when making an investment decision. At the end of the day, you can be confident that you made the right call based on the analytics which you have used to base your investment decisions.

So, let's jump right in!

Tool #1: The Three-Statement Model

This model lives up to its name.

It is based on the analysis of a company's financial statements. Hence, the name "three statement model" refers exactly to this type of model.

To conduct the right analysis, you will need to have the following financial statements: balance sheet, profit and loss, and cash flow statement.

In this model, what you are doing is essentially linking all three statements so that they make sense of the company's financial situation. You can use this model to get an accurate idea of a company's overall financial position. If the numbers show health financials, then you can feel that the company is in good shape and will produce good results down the road.

Now, the way this model works is that you will find a way to link all three statements into one model. What you can do is take the trend of each statement and look at the way they all move together. So, if all three statements show a trend for growth, then you can be sure that the company is in good shape.

However, if one the balance sheet is growing, but the profit and loss and the cash flow show signs of trending in the opposite direction, you would need to figure out why this is happening. There could be some unexpected situations, but the company is still solid.

If the company is posting profits, but their balance sheet is taking a hit, then you can assume that their financials are out of whack. In this case, you would really have to evaluate if this investment is really worth it. Perhaps it might, but a very short-term deal.

The use of this model is perfect for value investing and identifying the potential for a turnaround in a company that's been under water in recent history.

Tool #2: Initial Public Offering Model

An initial public offering (IPO) is the even in which a company switches from being a private company to be a publicly traded company. In this event, the company is valued at a certain price per share by that company's financial team, and then the IPO is underwritten by the bank, or investment firm, that is essentially sponsoring the IPO.

The issue here is determining the right IPO. This is based on the company's book value, and then a comparative analysis is conducted on the IPOs of other similar companies to see where your valuation can fit in.

When you conduct your comparative analysis, you need to consider a set of variables which can be compared among companies. For example, you can compare revenue, gross sales, number of employees, annual turnover, growth rate, and so on.

The actual variables which will be considered can all be compared in a large spreadsheet.

Then, each variable can be contrasted with the comparably-sized companies so that you can visualize if the results obtained correspond to the comparable.

If you find that your company is above the variables seen in most comparable, then you might be able to value your company at a higher per share price. If you see that it is below, then you might want to reconsider going public at that time. You might want to hold off going public at that time and wait until the company's financials improve.

Now, as an investor, the IPO valuation model is very useful since it allows you to see how individual companies stack against each other. This allows you to determine if your choice to invest in an IPO will make sense for you, or if you're better off waiting for the stock to prove itself in the market first.

However, I would like to recommend that you consider getting into IPOs whenever you have the chance since being one of the early stockholders can provide you with an opportunity to clean up when the stock takes off. As such, investors who get into the early stages of an IPO can position themselves for making good gains. This can happen when you understand the comparable of that company's IPO. You can see if the valuation makes sense, or if it's being valued too high. In which, you might want to wait to see what happens in the market first. If you see that the valuation is below comparable, then you might be looking at a potential bargain.

IPOs are great for position traders who might want to hold their position for some time while the stock gains tractions. Also, IPOs could be a great option for swing trading, particularly in the very early stages since the stock can heat up and get investors' attention quickly. You can flip your stock at some point in the early stages and make some decent returns.

Tool #3: The Revenue Model

This model consists in charting a company's revenue over a given period to see the trends in that company's revenue.

Earlier we discussed the importance of earning reports in determining the overall performance of a stock. As such, you can build a model for each company you are interested in trading based on its revenue.

The best way to build this model is to take its historical revenue reports, chart them and then calculate its trend line. You can do this on commercially available software such as Microsoft Excel, although your brokerage firm may offer you this type of analytics so you won't have to calculate it yourself.

So, how can you interpret this model?

Once you have charted the historical data for a company's revenue, you can then look at its trend and determine if it is growing or declining. I would recommend that you look at 10 years' worth of data since it will give you an accurate picture of where the company is going. This would be 10 years of quarterly reports. That means that you could have 40 different data points where you can contrast the company's trend.

With this model, you can see if the company is still expanding, leveling off, or declining.

When you see that a company's revenue is growing, you might consider it to be in an expansion phase. Depending on the age of the company, it could still be developing as part of its growth phase. If the company has been in the market for a longer period of time, say at least 50 years, you may want to take a look at older data, for example 25 years, and see if the company is having a renaissance due to factors such as management turnover, the introduction of new products, or a shift in market conditions.

This model is simple since it only looks the behavioral patterns of one variable over time, but it is the most powerful variable in stock trading. You can then overlay a company's revenue trend line with that of other economic variables such as Gross Domestic Product (GDP), inflation, consumer confidence, and major stock indices to see if the company is responding to the factors around it, or it is producing results in spite of the trends observed in the overall economy.

The best part of this model is that you can overlay as many variables as you like to get a sense of where that company's revenue is going as compared to any number of variables in its surroundings.

If a company has been publicly traded for less than 10 years, and there is no data available before its IPO, then you can take whatever data you have available and look at its revenue trend line. If you happen to see that the company has been posting positive results for each quarter it has been publicly traded, you might have a great company which you might want to hold on to for a longer period.

One other advantage of this model is that if a company misses its earnings expectations, and your chart that in this model, you might choose to dismiss one bad quarter as a one-off occurrence. Also, you might decide that it is a sign of things to come and it might be best to get out while you can.

Tool #4: The Forecasting Model

Industry experts will produce forecasts for companies' revenue.

These forecasts respond to the available data that analysts are looking at when determining where a company's earnings report should fall. These forecasts will produce an actual Dollar figure which estimates where that company's earnings report should fall.

Usually, forecasting is done on an earnings per share basis. This means that the per earnings per share price are calculated based on that company's track record and other variables which can be taken into account such as economic conditions affecting it, and any other variables which may come into play.

From that, analysts will produce a forecast where they expect that company's earnings per share to fall in line.

This is where analysts' expectations are bred. If the company beats analysts' expectations, the stock will soar. If the company does not meet expectations, then the stock will tank.

Here, you can create a model in which you can build a historical model which reflects that company's behavior regarding its ability to meet or exceed analyst expectations.

If you see that the company has a good track record of beating expectations, then you can be confident the company is on the way up. If it has a track record of missing expectations, there are one of two things going.

The first, analysts are missing something, and that is why they are getting their forecasts wrong. Or the second, the company is inconsistent and cannot produce results as expected by analysts.

Again, it's important to go as far back as you an in order to determine how companies have behaved historically. It could be that a company had a great track record and the began failing to meet expectations due to a management turnover. Or, this company may have been affected by adverse economic conditions such as changes in government regulation.

Whatever the case, your ability to determine a company's track record of meeting or exceeding forecasts will give you some wonderful insight into seeing where a company is headed. If you feel that the company is on the right track, you might have found yourself a go-to stock which you can even trade on a daily basis and make some solid returns.

Or, you might consider this stock as worthy of a longer-term investment especially around the time of earnings reports season. You can certainly make considerable profits when the company beats analyst expectations. However, don't ignore the company's fundamentals since you might pick up something that others have overlooked.

Tool #5: Resistance Level Model

This model takes the trend in moving averages to determine where "resistance" levels can be found. A found resistance level is a psychological barrier that investors and traders must pass in order to continue with the stocks trend.

Resistance levels are seen both at the top and the bottom, that is, both the floor and the ceiling of a stock.

If a stock is trending upward, you may often see that it won't pass a certain point. This would be a resistance level. And, it is often hard for a stock to break through a resistance level because investors may not feel comfortable with paying a certain price above a previous high.

In order to determine resistance levels, you need to look at the candlesticks of a stock and then compare it to its overall trend at the different points for moving averages. It could be that the 10-day moving average is trading in a given range, but it is not surpassing the high point of the 200-day moving average.

When you are in the presence of a resistance level, you can choose to approach the stock in a number of ways.

First, you can choose to day trade the stock within that range. For instance, you can set up a buy order when the price falls to the lowest point you have observed in its 10-day or 50-day trend. Then, you can set up your sell order when it hits the resistance level ceiling.

This strategy can help you make some decent if underwhelming profits. But as long as the stock doesn't break the resistance level, you can feel confident about trading within that range.

When the stock does break the resistance level, either as part the floor or ceiling, then you have to wait to see where the new high, or new low, will be set. You can follow the stock's ABCD pattern to determine where those new highs or lows will be set. Following this model will avoid you from being caught unawares by a stock looking to break a resistance level.

Also, there may be natural boundaries that investors are waiting for before attempting to break a resistance level. For example, investors may be waiting for key economic information, such as interest rate decisions by the Federal Reserve.

If rates are increased or cut, then the stock may break the resistance level due to investor's expectations. Whether the resistance level is the floor or ceiling, you need to be sure that, that resistance level will hold up over an extended period of time. If you are not sure about whether the resistance level may be broken, you might want to hold your position a bit longer when thinking about selling.

Likewise, if you are unsure if a stock will break the floor, then you can sit by patiently to see if it actually does. When it does break the floor, you can swoop in to pick up a great bargain. Otherwise, you may want to stay away from it until you have a better picture of where it is going.

Tool #6: The Gap Up Model

When stocks close on high at the end of a trading day, investors may be looking to continue pushing the stock upward at the opening of the next trading day. This is common when a company's report data in the afternoon of a trading day. Since they may report data at 2 o'clock pm, for example, that may not provide investors enough time to make the most of the stock's positive results.

As such, investors may choose to wait until the next trading day to pursue this stock. As a savvy day trader, you can purchase the stock right at the beginning of the trading day and wait for the gap to fill. When you hear that a "gap is filling," it means that the stock will go back to its previous highs after the euphoria has passed.

This is common when stocks rise due to psychological factors like a great news story being run on mainstream media. For example, XYZ corporation has been picked as the company of the year by a major news magazine.

This may lead investors to flock to that stock and try to get a piece of the action. However, the stock will encounter a resistance point somewhere and begin to fall back to Earth. The resistance level may trigger thousands of sell points and begin the price back down to its previous high in a hurry.

Now, you might find that that the stock may soon have a new floor, but that doesn't mean you can't lose money if you get in at the top and ride the wave back down.

You can play the gaps from one day to another, or over the weekends, by keeping your eyes and ears open about the way stocks are trending especially close to the end of a trading day.

Here, you can choose to keep a position open overnight and then watch out for when the gap is beginning to fill, or you can get in early at the beginning of the trading day. However, you may need to act quickly as you might miss a lower price point and you would have to get in at a higher price point.

Nevertheless, this type of trading is very short-term. When you are playing gaps, you should not expect to keep positions open for more than a few hours.

In fact, playing the gap may go as long as a full trading day, especially since the selloff, may be triggered in afternoon trading. Bear in mind that the selloff may occur due to traders closing their positions before the end of the trading day. So, you need to be aware that the stock may fall back to Earth in a matter of minutes.

As such, you must always keep your ears to the ground so that you can detect the oncoming trends.

A word of caution: when you are playing the gap, you can cash out when the stock is coming back down to Earth and the wait for it to settle at its new floor. When you see the new floor emerging, you can then pay attention to the candlesticks at this new resistance level. You might be able to determine a pattern which can lead you to continue trading that stock but at a new, higher resistance level.

Chapter 20 When is it Time to Sell for a Profit?

A milkman collects the milk from wholesalers and goes on to sell it in the markets and directly to the doorsteps of homes in Asian countries. Milk is a commodity that is bought and sold for profit. Milkmen sell it when the buyers are willing to buy it for a higher price. Will he sell it if there are no buyers or the price is half the price at which he bought it himself? The answer absolutely is a 'No.' Stocks are just like commodities. You buy them at a lower price and sell them to make profits when the demand is high.

When it comes to selling for profit purposes, the rule is simple: sell it when it still looks stronger and is on the high trajectory because this is the time when the demand is high and people are still interested in buying more of it. It will sell like hot cakes. This will save you from getting caught in periodical corrections in the stock market. Once you get caught in a correction, you waste money by wasting your time.

That's why if you are selling it early, it is even better. Most investors are looking forward to selling when the stock reaches the top price. Well, a few lucky dudes may find it at the top, but they also fail to sell it because they expect it to get higher. That's how almost no one becomes able to sell it at the top price. Be content with the gains you can make while the stock is still strong. Pull out of the bargain at an earlier stage. The key here is to stay calm, think logically, and never get excited as the stock shoots up.

The key to making money is selling soon. That's how you get protection from losses and that's how you succeed in accumulating money steadily. Steadiness is more important than speed.

Don't Sell Too Early

I have told you not to hold too long that the stock returns towards correction. So, when do you sell a stock for the maximum benefit? Where it is a mistake to wait too long to sell, it is also a mistake to sell it too early. You will be deprived of the profits you deserve the most. The universe works on the principle of balance. The sun rises in the east and sets in the west giving way for the moon to shine. Too much sun or too much moon will push the earth towards malfunction. That's how life goes on. Sometimes we smile; sometimes we are sad. These contrasting emotions help use create balance in our lives. That's how the stock market goes. You have to create a balance in your transactions.

Some investors get too cautious and start selling the stocks before their price matures. In this way, they lose valuable profit. There are some warning signs to alert you of when you need to hurry and sell the stocks.

When fundamentals are failing: If a company's fundamentals, like sales, debt, and cash flow start to show signs of stress, this means that something has considerably changed that is going to negatively affect the price of the stock. This is a warning sign. Don't wait for the market to panic over a decline in revenue. That's the point at which you need to unload that stock in profit.

When a stock has hit its target price: Set an upper limit at which you will sell. You must enter the upper limit price in you red diary that I have already asked you to carry with you. When the stock reaches its upper limit, sell it right away. Keep in your head that the stock will not move past your set target price, and that a single hint of any bad news will set the stock tumbling so that you are not tempted to hold it until the breaking point when it starts reversing. It is always better and recommended to take the returns you set at a target price, and then move on to other opportunities. Don't set the target price too high or too low. Sell it when it hits the target price and bag the profit to invest in other favorable situations.

Sell it when the company starts cutting dividends: when the company you have invested in starts cutting dividends, maybe the time is ripe to seriously consider selling it. Cutting the dividends is a serious issue, and it can have a drastic impact on the price of the stock. In most cases, it suggests financial issues on the company's end. So beware! Keep a close eye on it and get out in time.

Top Points to Selling

These are some of the important points to consider when you are selling the stocks.

You have bought a stock during the bullish period, and there is a wild selling streak. This selling is most likely uninformed and temporary and not as large as it appears to be. Top stocks indulge in sharp sell-offs for a couple days and even weeks. It is just a normal pull back. Don't freak out.

If you are looking to sell a stock, you need to keep in mind the trade volume of the particular stock. The ultimate top of a stock may happen on the day when the stock has the heaviest volume since it began advancing. You need to sell if a stock advance seems to be over active and having a rapid price rise for two to three weeks. The activity is known as climax top activity.

If a stock is running up, there are enough buyers in the market to absorb the shares that are sold. In addition, if there is a positive article published in a business newspaper or magazine, it is time to sell and bag profits. Beware if the volume is low, no matter how high the price bar reaches. Sell the stock right away. When buyers are overly optimistic, you definitely need to sell it. It means people are talking it up and asking everyone else to buy the stock to raise the price. But in reality, the price has reached its heights. Pull out early.

If the price of a stock fares badly on the index for multiple days, there is something fishy going on; sell it. It is an indication of a weak stock if it takes off making a good advance and then loses all the advance. Once you have reaped enough profit, sell it.

Sell if the other members of the same group don't show reasonable growth. But remember that there are lots of negative news circulating the markets. Don't fall for it. Never sell a potential stock on the basis of rumors that are most of the time intended to trigger an indiscriminate selling streak that will ultimately benefits the big fish. If you miss out on the top price or your target price, sell the stock on its way down. Make it fast.

If the stock declines 15% or more from the peak level, sell it. It may very well be an indication of weakness. Learn from the past selling mistakes. Be wiser. Make a chart in the red diary and analyze when to sell if you are facing an uncertain situation. Do your own post-analysis by drawing your own past buy-and-sell points. Don't wait until the stock has broken its support level. Selling after that is a poor decision because the stock will attract investors and aim for the higher end.

Chapter 21 Value Investing

People who invest in stocks usually have the same objective and that is to defeat the market. If you are really serious about being successful in investing in stocks, you should take the time to study and follow the proven strategies used by successful investors such as Warren Buffett, Benjamin Graham, and Seth Klarman.   These value investors have one secret strategy that has brought them success over the past decades.

For you to better to understand that secret strategy, let's talk about it in the context of shopping. Let's say that you and your family regularly consume soda so you regularly keep stocks of soda in your pantry. If you are a wise shopper, you will know that it is not the best time to buy a twelve-pack carton of soda when it is sold at $10. You know that the twelve-pack sodas is really worth $10 but you also know that if you are patient enough to wait for the right timing, you can buy the same twelve-pack at a discount. You will also know that the right time is not when the twelve-pack sodas are put on sale and sold for $7. You know that you can still get it at a cheaper price so you patiently wait until they become $4 a pack. When that opportunity comes, you will buy several packs to last you a couple of months or perhaps even for the rest of the year. You will get to enjoy your soda without paying the full price of $10. This strategy is basically what successful investors apply when they do value investing. They look for a stock whose current market price is way lower than its inherent value.

You must have heard about the complicated investment strategies that some expert investors use. Don't worry, though, for value investing is very effective but it is not at all complicated. To be successful, you do not need to have extensive experience in finance, avail of those costly online services, or learn how to interpret complex charts. To be successful, all you need are common sense, persistence, investment capital, and, of course, the eagerness to learn and perform some accounting. Before we continue with discussing the value investing strategy, we need to make sure that you have full understanding of the following underlying concepts about the strategy:

1. Companies Have Their Own Inherent Worth

The idea behind value investing is not really complicated and for all you know, you may have already been doing it in your own life. Value investing basically requires you to learn the real value of a particular investment so that you will know when it is being sold for much lesser than its actual value.

You will concur if you have been told that whether you purchase a new computer at a discount or at its full retail price, you will still take home the same computer with the same specifications and the same features. It is rather evident but let's just drive at the point we are making here. The value of that new computer will not really be reduced even if there are now better computers in the market. Well, stock investments are basically the same. The price of a particular stock may change even if the inherent worth of the company who owns the stock remains the same. Stocks, like computers, undergo a cycle wherein there are high and low demands. These changes in demand affect the prices of stocks but they don't really alter the value of what you are getting.

Smart consumers will not really buy a computer or any other electronic gadget at their full retail price because they know that these electronic gadgets normally go on sale during different times throughout the year. Stocks are basically the same, but the big difference is that you cannot really predict when stocks will go on sale. As is the case with most electronic gadgets, you know that retailers normally give out huge discounts during specific times of the year such as Black Friday. If changes in stock prices are as predictable as that, the demand for the stocks will increase which can in turn drive the prices up. To be successful in your stock investments, you must always be on the lookout for these "secret" sales and grab the opportunity before other investors find out about it.

2. Always Make Sure that You Have a Margin of Safety

When you buy stocks at discounted prices, you have a higher chance of making a profit when you finally sell the stocks. In case the prices of the stocks decline further, you will not lose that much money. This concept called margin of safety is actually used by many successful investors.

Let us look at an illustration for you to better understand this concept. If you know that the value of a particular stock is $10 and you get the opportunity to purchase it for $6, you can earn a profit amounting to $4 if you can patiently wait for the price to go back up to $10 which is its real value. It will still even be better when the company's operations expand because the stock of the company will become more valuable and the price may even go up to $20 or more. If that happens, you will earn $14 in unrealized gains for each stock that you have bought.

Benjamin Graham, one of the most successful investors who implemented value investing, made it his principle to only buy a stock when its current market price is 2/3 or less than its inherent worth. That was the margin of safety that Benjamin Graham used as his guideline in ensuring that he will get the most returns from his investments.

3. The Efficient-Market Hypothesis is Misleading

Many investors believe in the efficient-market hypothesis which basically says that the current market price of a particular stock represents the current value of the stock. Contrary to that hypothesis, value investors know that the current market price of a particular stock can be over or under its real value. For instance, a stock may have a low market price because the performance of the economy in general is poor and investors are starting to panic and sell their stocks. On the other hand, a particular stock may have a high market price because everybody is highly excited about the new technology that the company is working on but without the 100% guarantee that it will succeed.

4. Successful People Don't Follow What Everybody is Doing

Well, you can say that value investors who become successful are contrarians; they do not do what everybody else is doing. When they see that all the other investors are buying stocks, they will decide to sell theirs or just choose to do nothing. When all the other investors are selling their stocks, the successful value investors will start buying or maintain their existing portfolios and not sell. Value investors don't go with the flow and buy the most popular stock that a lot of people are raving about. Usually, these popular stocks have high market prices. Instead, they take their time to evaluate different stocks and they have the willingness to purchase a stock even if it is not popular or commonly bought by other investors, as long as they meet some specific criteria. The primary factor that value investors look at is the stock's inherent worth and not its popularity.

5. You Need Patience and Persistence in Order to Succeed

This may be the most important concept you need to understand. If you want to succeed as a value investor, you need to look at your investment from a long-term perspective. You should not expect to earn huge profits from your investments overnight. The reality is you may need to wait five to ten years before you can see any significant earnings from your investments. There will be times when you think that you are losing money and you would want to cash out in order to cut your losses. You need to remind yourself about your reasons for buying those stocks in the first place. If the stocks still meet the criteria you set for choosing them, you need to tell yourself to stay still and wait for the bad times to pass. Similarly, there will be times when you will hear other investors selling their stocks because the prices are high and you will be tempted to sell your stocks as well. You need to have the discipline to stick with your investment philosophy and strategy so you will not be tempted to do what other investors are doing.

How Stocks Become Undervalued

There are thousands, if not hundreds of thousands, of people who invest in the stock market but only a small percentage succeeds in the endeavor. Many stock market investors rely solely on their gut feelings and emotions when making investment decisions instead of performing diligent evaluations that can allow them to rationally decide whether a particular stock investment is good or not. They look at what other investors are doing and they decide to buy stocks even when the prices are continuously rising. They assume that the stocks are very good just because many people are buying the stocks and they want to make sure that they will get to enjoy the profits that the other investors are enjoying. They even regret not investing sooner because they think that the one- or two-month delay in their purchase already means lost profits for them. They feel that if they purchase as much as they can now, they will be able to ride with the stocks' success.

The same herd mentality is apparent when the stock prices start to plummet. When investors hear other investors are selling their stocks because of the poor performance of the stock market in general, they feel squeamish and they start to feel like they need to start selling their stocks, too. They are afraid that they might lose all their investments if they don't cash out now and they don't want to always have that uncertain feeling. This behavior is actually one of the biggest factors why stock prices continuously plummet which eventually affects the whole stock market.

Chapter 22 How to save huge on blue chip stocks

One of the best ways to profit during a market crash is to utilize cash secured put options on blue chip stocks. Now if you aren't aware what options are, they are contracts that give you the right, but not the obligation to buy or sell a stock at a certain price, at a certain date.

If you don't have previous experience with options or options trading then I recommend staying away until you are more familiar but if you do, they are a useful tool to have in your arsenal during a market downturn. Essentially you make a cash offer on a stock at well below the market rate. This the equivalent of finding a beautiful property in a great location and then making a lowball offer to buy it should it ever hit the market. Your offer may never be taken up, but if it is, you've just secured a great deal on a premium property, and now you can apply this same strategy to stocks.

Now I should note at the outset that any trading with "options" in the name has a certain amount of stigma within the investing community. We are not talking about riskier naked put options here, but a more conservative investment strategy. If you believe in the long term potential of the stock, but think there will be a dip in the price in the short term, then cash secured put options are a great way to capitalize on this.

Essentially you have a right, but not an obligation to buy these stocks at the lower price.

Your worst case scenario here is that you own a stock you previously wanted to own at a lower price. As these are blue chip stocks that we believe in the long term potential of, we are not assuming the traditional risk of the stock going to zero yet being obligated to buy at the higher price. However, this is still lower than the loss you would have taken if you had just purchased the stock outright at the higher price in the first place. Alternatively, the option expires worthless if the stock is still above the strike price at the date the option expires and you make a premium on the option itself in the short term.

For example, if Coca-Cola (currently trading at $43) is on your radar, you can wait until the price drops to $36 and then make an offer to buy at $33. This gives you a chance at a 25% discount from the current price and then sets you up for a strong long-term position in one of the world's most well-known brands.

The one important thing to remember with cash secured puts is that you must have enough liquidity in your account to cover the entire trade. 1 option equals a minimum of 100 shares so be sure of this before you execute any trades.

Chapter 23 Why you should consider short selling stocks

Shorting has long been a technique that the consumer level investor has overlooked and left to the "big boys" on Wall Street. For those of you unfamiliar with the term, short selling or "shorting" just refers to betting against a stock. So essentially you are betting that the stock will go *down* instead of up.

How the technical process works is that you borrow a certain number of shares from the original owner, then you sell your position the same way you would normally buy stocks, except you are selling instead of buying. At the consumer level, your brokerage platform does this automatically for you when you enter a short trade.

Some people have a moral opposition to shorting because they feel it is bad form to want a certain company's share price to go down. Really though all you are doing is spotting overvalued businesses or ones who business model is flawed in one way or another. This is how a few select investors got rich by shorting Enron in 2000. The most famous example, which is fantastically documented in the movie *The Big Short,* is Michael Burry's Scion Capital fund which began shorting the housing market in 2005 and made huge profits from the subprime mortgage crisis in the next 3 years. Burry was mocked at the time, yet his fund made investors over 400% returns in under 8 years, with his housing market bet one of the most profitable calls.

Now, I'm not suggesting you start shorting everything in sight. This would be a great way to lose money in the long term. However, shorting can be a useful hedge in terms of market turmoil, and will negate some of the losses that your portfolio will no doubt suffer.

Knowing when to short is key, and there is one pattern you should familiarize yourself with to capitalize on this opportunity. This is known as the "lower high" pattern. This is when a stock has rebounded after a dip but then peaks at a lower level than the previous peak before reversing once more. This signifies that the market is turning and we are in for a prolonged downturn.

Obviously the lower high can potentially come before a higher high, so you should set a hard stop loss above your initial short position, this is so your losses are minimal if the market does continue to rise.

If this all sounds complex, you can actually buy shorting ETFs. The two easiest ones are the ProShares Short QQQ (PSQ) which acts as an inverse of the Nasdaq 100, and the ProShares Short Financials (SEF) which acts as an inverse of the Dow Jones financial index. In other words, when these indexes go down, share prices of these ETFs go up.

For example, in the 2008 crash, the PSQ was up 69% in a little over 3 months. Just a small position in this would have saved your big losses on other parts of your portfolio.

Chapter 24 Stocks that traditionally do well during market downturns.

If you're not holding some of these, they are a great hedge when the market turns bad. Others are also solid, low risk, long term holds regardless of market conditions.

Retail

The first group of these are the giant low-cost retailers, ones that sell pretty much everything under the sun. The reason for this is demand for everyday items doesn't waver much during recessions. On top of this, those who traditionally shop at higher end retailers are hit, and therefore take their business to these lower end stores. Walmart is the big one of these, during the 2008 crisis, Walmart sales grew by 6.5% and stock prices rose 10.5% on the year, all while the S&P 500 dropped by over 30% in the same time period.

Following on from this you have the bargain basement retailers. These stores absolutely thrive when people are stretching their dollars. One such stock is Tanger Factory Outlet Centers, and their performance can be summed up in the words of CEO Steven Tanger "In good times, people love a bargain, and in tough times, people need a bargain." Outlet stores like these are also less prone to having their market share eaten away by ecommerce. If there's one area that Amazon hasn't yet penetrated, it's the deep discount market across all sectors. Consumers will still head out to their local discount store to get the cheapest toilet paper and snacks, rather than order them online.

Dollar Tree is another one stock that falls into this category and has boasted strong performance in market downturns. Discount clothing retailer Ross was yet another stock that significantly outperformed the S&P in 2008. These both could represent solid plays if you're looking to recession-proof your portfolio.

Resources

When stocks go South, resource commodities go in the other direction. Gold, silver and other mining companies thrive during bad economic periods as demand for their commodities increases. In fact, since the rise of cryptocurrencies, both the silver to gold and platinum to gold ratio are at all time lows. Both of these commodities traditionally perform very well in recessions, are tremendously undervalued at this time, and as such mining firms for these should certainly have a part in your portfolio. What's more is, the market tends to overreact to the companies themselves when you look at company valuations vs. Valuations of the commodity they are mining. Therefore a 30% increase in gold prices could see a 50% increase in the share price of mining companies.

Precious metals have always been a global hedge against currency deflation and market crashes, and it is unlikely anything will change regarding this during the next recession.

Relaxation

You're probably thinking, "what the hell is this guy talking about?, who on Earth is relaxing during a market crash?" Well then answer me this, why did Anheuser Busch InBev grow by 39.4% in 2008? They provided the cheapest mass market beer, which in turn provides self medication and a brief escape from reality from many folks who are down on their luck. No matter what the economic conditions look like, people are still going to drink.

Even though this was the year when Anheuser Busch was bought out by InBev, revenues still grew by 5% from the previous year. Then we have the big entertainment stocks like Disney and Viacom, which also tend to do well during the lean years, because people still watch TV and although they may cut back their movie spending, that tends to be more of the Mom & Dad date night movies than the family friendly ones, which still receive decent box office numbers. After all, there's no way people aren't taking their kids to see the latest Avengers or Thor movie.

We can also add adult entertainment to this. The adult industry thrives during these years, as more people spend nights in than out of the house. Unfortunately, from a social perspective, porn usage rises with unemployment. So with increased lay offs during recessions, we also see increased click rates on adult websites, and increases in share prices of many of the adult entertainment companies.

Others

As well as stocks that thrive, we have the market neutral industries such as health care, and pharmaceuticals, as well as, tax prep services and life insurance companies. No matter what the prevailing market conditions, people will always have to do certain things. These are paying their taxes, then they will get sick, and then they will die. Usually in that order, but not always. These stocks tend not to be affected by whether the economy is going up or down and often make decent long-term holds because of this.

Chapter 25 Identifying and Picking the Right Growth Stocks

To recap, growth stocks are stocks that may not necessarily have strong fundamentals. Regardless, the stock market, for better or worse, somehow fell in love with these stocks. If you need a great example of a growth stock, take a look at Facebook or Tesla. Compared to other companies with stronger fundamentals, it's usually a no-brainer comparing the stocks of these high flying and heavily hyped companies with more solid companies.

In normal times, people would pick stocks that have zero to no debt, solid sales growth, industry domination and solid management as well as tremendous cash flow. Unfortunately, or fortunately, depending on your perspective, the stock market values stock primarily in terms of perceived growth potential. This is how stocks like Twitter were able to achieve some traction early on before gravity pulled them back down to earth.

One big danger with growth stocks is that, eventually, the stock market may fall out of love with you. That's the bottom line. When that happens, reality hits. It's as if scales fall out of people's eyes and they notice the huge amount of debt the company has. They start noticing that the company only has two or three major customers. They realize the company's cash flow over a four-quarter period actually goes through some tremendous turbulence.

Unfortunately, if you're one of those investors who realize this later on after the stock has tanked, you're pretty much a day late and a buck short. Keep this in mind when it comes to growth stocks.

I don't mean to discourage you but we need to be clear as to what exactly we're looking at. These are not, generally speaking, fundamentally strong stocks.

With that said, one of the techniques that I will teach in this chapter involves using fundamental analysis to pretty much separate growth stocks in terms of likely winners and probable losers. Before we begin, let's do a quick recap.

What are Growth Stocks?

Growth stocks are shares of companies that appreciate faster and higher than general market indices like the Dow Jones Industrial Average index.

For example, the Dow Jones Industrial Average appreciates 20% year after year, you can bet that growth stocks leave that in the dust. We're talking maybe doubling in a year or possibly doing much better. Whatever the case may be, there is a big black and white difference between general index performance and growth stock performance.

Also, when you pay attention to the other stocks in these growth companies' industries, they leave everybody behind. It's as if they are the Cinderella story of their particular industry.

Again, Tesla Motors is a good example of this. Usually, when people think of the automotive industry in the United States, they think of companies like Ford, General Motors, and others. But Tesla shines in this industry. It's as if gravity doesn't work on that stock. It seems that the normal rules that hold back and drag down automotive stocks don't apply to Tesla. It's as if investors hold it to a different standard.

It's easy to see why, because the resume of its CEO, Elon Musk, is more reminiscent of Silicon Valley and its high-flying tech stocks than Detroit and the old industrial America that pretty much characterizes the US automotive industry.

Also, when you look at the specific underlying technology of Tesla, you really can't say that it is purely an automotive company. If anything, it's an electric motor vehicle organization.

With that said Tesla is a growth stock because its rate of appreciation sets it apart and puts it head and shoulders above its competitors, both in its industry as well as in terms of the general industrial average. Keep this in mind when determining which stock, on its face, is a growth stock and which stock isn't.

Invest in Growth Stocks to Grow Your Wealth

What good are growth stocks for? If you are faced with two opportunities: investing in a solid company that dominates in its industry, has solid cash flow and is never in the red, or a company that just got started and admittedly gets a lot of media hype and love, which should you choose?

Well, it really boils down to what your objectives are. If you are looking for long term growth because you are investing your retirement money, chances are, you should go with solid companies with solid fundamentals. These are companies that are not going anywhere anytime soon.

On the other hand, if you're younger or you just graduated from college and got your first corporate job, your objectives and mindset might be different. You might be in a hurry to grow whatever you managed to save in your 401K or IRA plan. If so, you might want to take a long, hard look at growth stocks because they are great for quick portfolio growth.

How much growth? We're talking about out-pacing the general market indices. Whether you're comparing your stock's growth to the S&P 500, the Nasdaq or the Dow Jones Industrial Average, you can bet that if you pick the right companies, you can get solid returns.

Before you get too excited...

It's easy to understand the concept of growth stocks but picking out the right stocks is another matter entirely. So how exactly do you tell which growth stock is worth investing your hard-earned dollars on?

What makes this complicated is that it's often hard to spot brand new growth stocks. These are stocks that, for the longest time, were just plodding along. They're basically just another company in the crowd. Not that many people are paying attention to them. Maybe only a handful of analysts would track their stock. All of a sudden, they start getting a lot of love and attention from the rest of the stock market.

It's hard to get in on growth stocks right at the point of ignition. It's easy to get in when they've already appreciated quite a bit. For example, Apple Computers was pretty much on its deathbed at certain levels during the period when Gil Amelio was the CEO of that Cupertino, California-based computer giant. The interesting thing about the Amelio period was that only a few people remember it. It was a time where Apple stocks were basically on life support.

And one of the best things that Apple did at that time was to buy out Steve Jobs' company, Next. Apple wanted Next not because of its computers, which was sold through a very narrow education-based marketing channel, but because of its operating system.

It turned out to be the defining point in Apple Computer's corporate history because the second act of the Steve Jobs era brought the iPod, the iPhone, the iPad and key innovations that blew up Apple stock to the stratosphere. But you would not have seen that coming when you saw how Apple's stock performance was plodding along at the end of John Sculley and Gil Amelio's leadership periods.

This is a classic example of a growth stock. If you owned Apple stocks at its lowest point at that period, you'd be a very, very wealthy person today. Apple has just basically blown up ever since that point, thanks to the amazing growth made possible by the iPhone.

I tell the story of Apple because it's easy to relate with that story. We're talking about a real company with real products producing real changes. Make no mistake about it, for better or worse, the iPhone and the age of consistent Internet connection changed the world.

Indeed, it was a fulfillment of CEO Steve Jobs' challenge to John Sculley when he hired Sculley from Pepsi. He said, to paraphrase, "You can spend the rest of your life selling sugared water, or you can change the world." And sure enough, Apple Computers changed the world.

Now, it's easy to see how Apple would be a growth stock, but I've got some sobering news. The vast majority of growth stocks out there are not of the same caliber as Apple. A lot of them are simply creatures of hype or market reputation. Whatever the case may be, the dollars that you make when you buy these stocks low and you unload them for a high price is all too real.

In other words, you make the same real dollars trading these stocks as if you had traded Apple stocks.

The key here is to buy the right stocks before the rest of the market recognizes that the stock that you're buying is actually a growth stock. This is how you position yourself to become wealthy. As the old saying goes, you make your money when you buy.

Usually, when people think about earning a profit, they think about making the money when they unload. That's wrong. You make your money when you buy. In other words, you recognize the value that is unnaturally low or isn't being fully recognized by the rest of the market. This is the same philosophy that animates Warren Buffet's investment strategy. It's all about looking at unrecognized or unappreciated value.

How do you go about picking the right growth stocks?

Step #1: Compare stock growth over the same time frame with a broad index

For example, you're trying to determine out of a basket of 100 stocks which of these would make for a growth stock. You look at their individual performance over a fixed period of time and find the broad index growth rate. Whether we're talking about the S&P 500 or the Nasdaq or Dow Jones Industrial Average, it doesn't really matter. You would see which of these in a basket of 100 stocks grow at a very decent rate compared to the index.

Step #2: Compare stock growth over the same time frame to their industry's average

Now that you have filtered your initial basket of stocks, the next step is to look for their industry's indexes and compare their stock's growth over the same time frame. Again, after this step, you should be able to filter out some stocks from your list.

Step #3: Consistent stock growth over a significant time frame

What constitutes a significant time frame? Usually, 3-5 years is a good comparative time frame. Don't get too crazy with extending this too far back because the company, 5 years ago, might be a fundamentally different company and it would not make much sense to compare the company now to what it was before.

Maybe it was in a different industry, maybe it was run by a different CEO, and maybe it had a different philosophy. Whatever the case may be, 5 years is a good enough time frame. Extending it way past that period might be counterproductive.

The key here is just to find some sort of consistency. We're talking about quarter over quarter growth, both in sales, earnings and stock price.

Step #4: Filter by P/E

Now that you have a fairly short list, the next step is to filter your list based on price per earnings ratio.

For example, if a stock is making $10 per share of profit and its current stock price is $200, its P/E is 20. Now, what is the upward limit of your P/E filter? 40 is a good cap. If you find a stock that is beyond 40, you might want to skip it.

Usually, the lower the P/E, the more attractive the stock. Anything under 40 means that there is still a way to go for the stock to appreciate. If you are looking at a stock that is already at 40 or close to 40, it's pretty much maxed out. Unless, of course, its earnings continue to grow at a healthy clip. This earnings growth could justify a higher stock price.

Step#5: Compare growth stock candidates among the percentage of institutional owners

This filter requires you to get to the nitty gritty of the company's SEC filings. The US Securities and Exchange Commission requires public companies to make a public filing of their percentage of institutional owners. In other words, how much of all their stock holders are pension funds, mutual funds, investment banks and other professional institutional shareholders. At this point, you're going to try to filter based on a percentage of ownership. The higher the percentage, the better.

The reason for this is actually quite simple. When an institution buys millions of stocks in a company, it usually locks in a fairly long period of time-especially if they get a decent return. In other words, they don't freak out like an individual investor and liquidate their positions just because the stock experiences hiccups

Usually, they would stay for quite some time due to bureaucratic and institutional reasons. This provides quite a bit of stability. At the same time, this also makes the stock more attractive to other institutional owners because, usually, institutions tend to behave with a herd mentality. If they see that a lot of "smart money" is investing in one particular company, a lot of them would also want invest. But since they hold billions of dollars in assets, you can see that they can move quite a bit of stock and this can lead to some serious appreciation due to the volume involved.

Step #6: Consistent sales growth

Pay attention to a potential growth stock's financial filing. Look at whether its underlying sales are actually growing year over year. Usually, 10% appreciation is a nice benchmark. The more the better. What's important is its consistency.

In other words, it's okay if a company isn't appreciating 10% or more year after year in sales growth, as long as it is marching forward. In other words, in one year, it's 10%, and then it's 11% and 12% and so on and so forth. There can be dips, but as long as it's over a 10% threshold, this is a good sign.

Steer clear of companies that have flat sales or sinking sales. This can indicate a lot of things. Either they only have a small number yet high-volume customers, or their industry is changing. It may well turn out that it's only hype or reputation keeping the company's stock up.

Don't be the investor who is left holding the bag when you bought in on hype and it turns out that the company's sales have been hemorrhaging for the past few years. Again, when doing sales growth analysis, keep it within a time frame that's manageable like 3-5 years.

Step #7: Track earnings growth
Look at the sales growth at Step #6 and pay attention to the total earnings of the company. Does it keep up with sales growth? Does it have a decent tracking with sales growth or does the company's earnings and sales go on opposite directions?

Step #8: Decreasing or low debt
Pay attention to how much debt a company has. Again, by law, American public companies release this information, so you should look into the financial statements of the company and look for its debt load. In particular, pay attention to its year over year debt level. Is it decreasing or does it maintain a fairly low amount of debt? On the other hand, is its debt load swelling?

Extra Research

Just in case you haven't tired of the 8 Steps listed above and you still have a lot of spare time, here is some extra research that you should do in determining whether your initial basket of potential growth stocks yields some gems.

Is the company a market leader? Pay attention to its market and see whether it's in the top 3. Analyze its industry and try to figure out if the industry is growing or undergoing a massive sea change.

Keep in mind that, thanks to technology, a lot of industries have been disrupted. For example, the compact disc industry is fairly small compared to its former self. The same applies to all sorts of optical media like DVD discs. Pay attention to the state of the industry. Is it undergoing disruption or is it growing?

Also, pay attention to the branding of the stock. As I've mentioned earlier, oftentimes, what separates a high-flying stock from what would otherwise be a solid company that doesn't trade all that well is the amount of media mentions it has and how much the rest of the market has fallen in love with that stock. Pay attention to its brand. Does it have a solid brand? Is there massive market buzz?

Usually, when you detect this, this is reflected in the stock's price already. However, if you notice that there's not much market buzz around the company's products or it has few media mentions, you might have a gem in your hands if it has solid brands and a low stock price. You might be looking at an undiscovered or fairly obscure growth stock that may have a breakout point in the future.

Next, pay attention to its product line. Does the company have new products in the pipeline? How important are patents in the company's industry? Are we talking about a company that basically has mature product lines that may even go off patent? Pharmaceutical giants are the first ones that come to mind when it comes to this type of analysis.

Finally, does the company look like it's poised for market domination? Does it have a certain sub-niche that we can reasonably say it's either poised to take over or it has already taken over but the market hasn't caught on yet?

Again, with all these filters that I've given you, you should have more than enough to go with in terms of figuring out which company it might be on the brink of a nice stock breakout. Breakouts happen when the rest of the stock market starts paying attention to a company because the market finally wakes up to the tremendous amount of value the company brings to the table.

The next step, of course, is to buy in and hold growth stocks for short term to mid-term gain. The key to growth stocks is you should not hold them forever unless they have become blue chip stocks or they have really solidified their position that they make for great fundamental long-term plays.

Remember to Switch From Growth Stock to Growth Stock

Keep in mind that what makes a growth stock a growth stock is the fact that there's a tremendous amount of market buzz around it. Please understand that the party is not going to last forever. The love affair is probably going to be short lived. Do yourself a big favor and be ready to switch from growth stock to growth stock.

You're chasing after return on investment. You're chasing after appreciation. You're not necessarily falling in love and getting married to the stock. It's not a long-term commitment. Be ready to hit the exit button.

The bottom line with growth stock is actually quite simple. You're just trying to hitch a ride on different stock's growth rate. If done right, don't be surprised if your portfolio appreciates by double digits or even triple digits year after year.

Chapter 26 The Basics of Fundamental Investing

Fundamental investing really boils down to investing in a company because you believe in what the company is doing and its potential. This requires a lot more work than technical trading.

With technical trading, your data points basically begin and end with the performance of the stock. Now, your data set can extend for a long time in the past and can be projected quite some time in the future, but it only comes from one place. It only comes from the actual performance of the stock. There is no other source of data points. This gives you a greater sense of control.

With fundamental investing, you're focused on three key questions. Is the company making money? Will it continue to make money in the future? How well does it compare to others in its industry?

Now, it may seem that these questions are pretty simple and straightforward, but it really boils down to how you get information to answer these questions. Many analysts could try to answer these questions regarding a particular company and come up with completely different answers.

Fundamental investing, ultimately, is all about the midterm to long term value of the company. It's not really the stock itself that you're paying attention to, but the company's quality, how well it's doing, and how likely it is that it would do better in the future.

Another key aspect of fundamental investing is that you are looking for bargains. That's the bottom line. Either you are looking for a company that is underpriced by the market now or in the future.

It's easy to understand the first scenario. For example: Company A is doing really well in its industry. It is a market leader, has great products in its development pipeline, and possesses a tremendous client base. Still, it's in an industry that is, for some reason or other, not very sexy. Similarly, its growth rate is not as stunning as internet companies or other technology-based companies.

While this company is making more money than companies in sexier industries, it doesn't matter to the market. The market thinks that this company is simply just not interesting enough. However, when you look at the cash flow of the company, how much debt it has, and all other important factors, you can see that there is a tremendous amount of discounting going on as far as its market valuation. There's a big disconnect between what its stock price should be based on its earnings and earnings potential and what the company currently trades at.

The analysis above estimates the hidden value of the company as it stands now. There is also another way to do fundamental investing: forecasting a company's future worth.

Warren Buffet and other legendary investors often work this way. They don't mind paying a premium for a company now because they are so confident that the company is going to perform even better in the future, that they're actually getting in at a discount. This is one aspect of fundamental investing that you should also pay attention to.

The Big Challenge in Fundamental Investing

Trying to find a discount now, as far as the actual value of the company as it exists now, is actually getting harder and harder. As more analysts and value investors flood the market, there is less and less of these 'undervalued' companies because the price per earnings ratio of these companies tends to get bid up.

Now, these fundamental stock plays are not going to be at the same level as growth stocks, but their prices do tend to get bid up. The better approach would be to disregard their high prices now because, based on your projections, you see this company being a bargain based on its future performance.

Fundamental Investing Goals

What are the goals of people who invest using a fundamental investing strategy? First of all, they buy stocks in companies with solid fundamentals that are either low priced now or can be justifiably bought now at a high price because of projected future growth.

It's still the same strategy. You're looking for some sort of "under appreciation." You're looking for some sort of discount. There has to be some sort of disconnect between what the company is truly worth and its price currently or its price in the future.

What are the Fundamentals of a Company?

The operative word in the phrase "fundamental investing," of course, is "fundamental." So what is so fundamental about "company fundamentals?"

First of all, you're going to use financial statements issued by the company. These are required by law from public companies. Officer of a public company are required to make public their financial statements.

As a fundamental investor, you're going to look through a company's quarterly and yearly filings. You would then get a clear idea of the company's quarterly and yearly revenue, its income, and its growth trend. You are also going to pay attention to its profit margin, as well as its debt load and return on equity.

What is Return on Equity?

Return on equity measures how much profit the company produces per dollar invested in the company. This highlights the fact that the company is able to turn whatever amount of money is invested in it and grow it by a certain rate. Now, the bigger the rate, the better.

How do we arrive at ROE or return on equity? Take the total amount of money invested in the company and divide it by the amount of profit generated by the company. This is your ROE.

It determines whether the company seems like it's making money but is actually burning through a lot of cash just to produce income, or it's an actual money generator. Because you know you are looking at a very attractive company when it takes a fairly low amount of cash and is able to multiply it. The more cash it generates from actual investment inputs, the better that company looks.

Pay Attention to the Company's Overall Ability to Produce Positive Cash Flow

Cash flow is one of the most important factors a fundamental investor looks at. In fact, Warren Buffet makes a big deal out of cash flow. If you determine that a company has a positive cash flow pretty much throughout the year, then you can be more confident in the company. You would know that this company does not suffer from structural or operational weaknesses that may put it at a serious disadvantage if certain conditions come to pass.

For example, if a company suffers certain cash flow bottlenecks consistently throughout the year, this may be due to the fact that most of its money is tied up in accounts receivables. As long as that money can be successfully billed from the companies and individuals who owe that money, then the company is going to be making money.

What if for some reason or other the company's industry suffers a downturn and institutional clients can't produce the cash? This is going to be a serious issue.

The good news is you can see this a mile away when you look at the cash flow figures of a company. You can see whether it has a wide base of customers. You can see whether it has a diverse range of customers across a few industries. You can also see whether there are structural limits to where its cash is coming from.

Make Earnings Estimates for the Future

Another aspect of fundamental investing is that you make earnings estimates for the future. You don't just look at what the company is doing right now. For all intents and purposes, chances are, the company's performance right now is already baked into its stock price. Instead, you're going to make an educated guess as to how well it would do in the future. Based on current earnings, you're going to project its earnings estimates into the future.

Of course, this is not as simple as it may seem. You can't just do a straightforward projection. For example, if a company grew by 5% in the past 10 quarters, it doesn't make sense for you to automatically assume that it's going to grow at that same rate. You have to factor in what's going on in the general economy, the health of the specific industry the company is in, the state of the competition, and the specific growth rate of the different parts of the company. In other words, the projection must be conditioned by other factors. Otherwise, you might just be fooling yourself into thinking that, since the company has grown steadily in the past, then this automatically means it will continue in the future.

Conditions do change. Often times, they change overnight. Don't automatically assume the same growth rate. Factor in realistic parameters.

Beware of Expert Earnings Estimates

If you think you might have a tough time making earnings estimates for a company you're thinking of investing in or a company that you have already invested in, wait until you look at the work of experts. There are many stock market experts and company analysts. In fact, there's too many of them.

The problem is, a lot of them are associated with or come from' prestigious' trading houses and investment banks that it's too easy to give too much weight to them. Many investors think that as long as the estimates are 'official' statements of well-respected investment banks, they should trust it automatically. You have to look through the numbers the 'experts' processed and see if you would come to the same conclusion.

The good news about these analyst reports is that they include all the numbers that they considered when coming to their conclusions. They open this information so anybody who has the time and attention to detail can check out those numbers for themselves. It is your job to see if the numbers reasonably support the conclusions of the analysts.

You have to do this yourself. At the very least, skim or scan through the materials. Don't just agree automatically.

Product Pipeline Considerations

Another key factor to consider when doing fundamental analysis is how broad the product pipeline of the company is. This is very important because there are many companies who are making a lot of money, but their product lines are mature. In other words, it's going to be a long time until a new crop of products replaces their top earners. This is a big issue for pharmaceutical companies and other industries where patents expire over time.

Pay attention to this issue because you might be stepping into a trap. You might be buying into a company that may be on its way to a long, painful decline. It may have started already. You think you're getting into this amazing multinational big brand pharmaceutical company, but it turns out that a lot of their blockbuster drugs are already turning generic or only have a few years left of patent protection.

Don't get caught by surprise. Make sure that the product pipeline of the company that you are thinking of buying is robust enough to sustain continued growth. In the case of pharmaceutical companies, be clear on their patent acquisition plans-if they can't come up with products on their own, they should have solid plans for buying smaller companies with promising patent applications or current products.

Balance Sheet Analysis

Balance sheet analysis really gets to the heart of the value of the company. Seriously. If there are any two pieces of official, legally mandated disclosures that you absolutely need to pay attention to as a fundamental investor, it's the balance sheet and cash flow analysis.

The balance sheet simply takes the company's liabilities and deducts it from the company's assets. What's left is shareholder equity or the net worth of the company. This gives you a big picture view of what this company is truly worth.

Management Analysis

Depending on how long you've been investing and how many manager profiles you've checked out, management analysis might be useful for you. Pay attention to how visionary the leadership is.

Please understand that in corporate America, corporate competence is assumed. In other words, a company's officers are presumed to already know how to do their jobs. The big issue is whether they have a good idea as to what to do. In other words, do they have vision? The bigger the company, the higher the chance that it's going to attract top notch operators. These are people who know how to do things.

The big question: are they being guided by top brass leadership to do the right things that would position the company for continued dominance in the future or position the company for even greater heights? How do you analyze this factor when selecting stocks?

First of all, pay attention to how visionary its leadership is. Look at their official 'vision' statements or other public 'vision' statements. Pay attention to the track record of the results the team produces. Take a look at whether the results tend to grow over time. Finally, pay attention to the CEO. How long has he or she been on the job?

If the CEO has been at the helm for a long time, then you should think about succession issues. Who is slated to replace the CEO? Again, apply the analysis above to the successors. How visionary are they? Do they have a track record of producing results?

Sales Analysis

It's also important to look at the overall sales of the company and see if it is growing on a quarter over quarter basis. Now, a few dips here and there are okay. However, the company should be growing and it should be growing at a robust pace. If not, chances are other companies would look more attractive by comparison.

Disclaimer: don't hang your hat on this. This is not the one answer that should make you buy a stock or skip it. However, it does lay the foundation as to whether the company has a future. If sales are growing at a healthy clip on a quarter by quarter basis, then, with everything else being equal, this is a company to pay attention to.

Operating Income vs. Actual Income

Another way fundamental investor dissect companies is to pay attention to their operating income and compare it to their actual income. Income analysis is extremely important. The good news is, by law, the securities and exchange commission in the United States, requires public companies to release income statements. This is called 10K and 10Q filings. Pay close attention to these documents.

These documents are presented in a fairly clear way. You just need to look at certain lines in the report. First of all, you need to look at the net income line. This will tell you the profit the company earned... This is net income.

Sounds pretty straightforward, right? Well, not quite. You have to pay attention to non-recurring income or extraordinary charges.

For example, it may seem that a company lost money for the quarter. It may even be a very big loss. But if the report states that it is a one-time charge because the company's laying off people or shutting down divisions, you need to look closer. Why? When you discount these extraordinary items, it may well turn out that the company is actually making money.

Similarly, if the company made a tremendous amount of money in the past quarter, take a look as to whether this is non-recurring income or an extraordinary windfall. Sometimes, companies get a huge infusion of cash because they sold off a division or they sold off some assets. This may seem exciting because the net income blew up, but when you discount those, it may well turn out that the company is bleeding money and not doing really well.

In order for you not to get thrown off by the net income line, you should focus instead on reading income statements with an eye towards operating income. This is actual income from normal operations.

By normal operations, we're not talking about selling a division of the company or selling assets or any one-time situation. We're also not talking about adjusting tax brackets, which can only be done infrequently. Instead, we're talking about normal income generating operations. This is how well the company usually does on a day to day basis.

One key shortcut to determining operating income is to pay attention to a reporting line that says "earnings before interest, taxes depreciation and amortization" or EBITDA. This should give you a clear idea of the operating income of the company you are analyzing.

Cash Flow Analysis

In addition to income analysis, cash flow analysis is one of the most important analyses you could do if you are pursuing a fundamental investing strategy. With cash flow analysis, you pay attention to net income versus cash flow.

Net income really boils down to total profit. Revenues minus costs. This is a problem because sometimes, it can hide expenses, depreciation or credit costs. Cash flow, on the other hand, makes it much harder to hide these things. It also makes it harder to hide structural weaknesses in the company.

With cash flow analysis, you get to measure temporary losses that fund all the operations. You get a clear idea of a company's obligations and debts as well as the promotions it does. This analysis gives you such a clear view of a company's prospects that you should look for companies that have enough cash to cover all debt. It should have enough resources to take care of all marketing and operations and have cash left over for additional future projects.

If you look at the cash flow statement of a company and it shows that the firm experiences negative cash flow (at least two times per year), this should be a red flag to you. This highlights the fact that the company might be suffering from structural issues. It still makes a profit overall, but this provides cold comfort because there are certain rough patches the company goes through every single year. If you don't see this and business conditions change, it doesn't take long for that negative cash flow to translate into a loss for the year.

Where does negative cash flow stem from? It can be due to a small customer base restricted to a narrow range of industries or is restricted to just one industry. It can also arise when only one customer accounts for almost all the sales of the company. Cash flow issues can reflect the fact that most of the products sold by the company are sold on credit. This is the accounts receivable scenario I described earlier. Finally, cash flow issues also tend to shed light on slow product development.

Be very suspicious and concerned if any of these are in play as revealed in the form of negative cash flow. This doesn't necessarily mean that you have to completely avoid the company or just give up on it. Instead, this should prompt you to dig deeper as to its fundamental value and see if there are any other points of attraction in the company.

Earnings Per Share Analysis

Take the total net income of the company and divide it by the total number of shares outstanding. This gives you an earnings per share figure. Now, the next step is to take the current price of the company's stock and divide it by the earnings per share. This gives you a price per earnings ratio.

Now, what do you do with this ratio? Well, it's all comparative. You look at other companies in the same industry as the company you're analyzing and make sure that they share the same fundamentals. You don't want to compare apples to oranges. You want to make sure that you're comparing pretty much similar companies who deal with the same fundamentals.

After you have lined up these companies, pay attention to their price/earnings ratio or P/E. This should highlight which companies are expensive, which companies are relative bargains, and what is the industry average P/E.

Once you have these figures, compare these numbers with the P/E of companies in the overall stock market. By doing all these comparisons, you should get a fairly clear idea as to whether a company is trading at a bargain or whether it's overbought or overvalued.

Cash Flow Per Share Analysis

Take total cash flow figures from the operations of the company and divide it by the shares outstanding. You then compare this figure with cash flow per share figures from other companies within the same industry. Again, this should give you a fairly clear picture of how that company stacks up to the competition in terms of investment potential.

Combine Cash Flow and P/E Analysis

The next step is to combine both the figures you get from your cash flow and P/E analysis to determine which stock is underpriced. Many stock experts say that cash flow analysis is the best way to value and compare stocks.

Once you reach this stage, you have all the data that you need to properly compare stocks. You can only tell if something is a bargain if you compare it to something else.

You have to line them up and see where the numbers fall. You can't just automatically assume that since the company reached a certain threshold that it is necessarily a good deal. Don't compare it with itself or compare it so some sort of abstract ideal. Compare it to other companies in its industry.

Look for strengths that a company has that others don't have. On the flip side, always look for weaknesses that it has that others don't have and cross reference these or support these with the financial numbers they are legally required to supply. Once you have everything together, you can then properly size up which companies are good deals and which ones are trading at a steep premium.

Chapter 27 Stock scanning and building a watch list

In this dynamic trading market, it is essential that you are on top of the most lucrative stocks and securities. However, with so many stocks, it is almost impossible to keep an eye on each one of them. This is where stock scanning can come in handy.

A stock scanner is software that will go through numerous stocks, instantaneously, searching for the precise criteria you would like to lookup. Without a scanner, you will have to skim through an endless stream of charts. This is difficult and exhausting. These scanners not only save energy but also save times. In short, they are game-changing software that no day trader should miss out on.

Starters

For starters, this tool is imperative because it will assist them in developing a watch list. So what exactly is that? A stock watch list is an enumeration of securities being observed for prospective trading or opportunities.

A day trader should create a watch list of dozens, or even hundreds of trading alternatives to ensure that they make an appropriate and informed investment decision. This list can assist the trader in staying abreast of monetary or other factors that could influence these assets, stocks, or securities.

Moreover, it will be a lot easier for you to remember the securities if they are being monitored someplace. When the stock price drops on some short-term bad news, you can purchase it for a steal.

As seen from successful traders, the battle when it comes to day trading revolves around choosing the right stocks. These right stocks are those tradable stocks which you are familiar with. It implies that you have properly researched their patterns and understand them fundamentally.

Watchlist

Creating a watch list is not enough. It has to be an effective one. This is where stock scanners play a vital role. These engines let you filter through thousands of stocks to recognize the prospects from each. All these stocks show up on a single page called Predefined Scans.

From the scans, you can pick out the most lucrative choices and invest in those securities. Using the predefined scans, day traders can discover stocks that they like and want to observe. Rather than having the stocks scattered and taking time to find it; stock scanners will help place them in one proper list.

Liquidity elements

In short, you would need to follow three steps to create an effective watch list. First, day traders have to gather liquidity elements in every main sector. Second, you will have to add scanned stocks (using scanners) that meet overall criteria with the market approach you adopt. Lastly, rescan the list every night to detect patterns or systems that possibly will yield opportunities in the upcoming session while rejecting stocks you don't think are feasible. You may discard some securities because of technical violations, secondary offerings, or even mergers.

In addition, for starters, you must keep the watch list restricted to 5-10 stocks only. Otherwise, you may get confused, and the outcome could possibly be a lot different than you expected. Over time, you can segment diverse watch lists.

Chapter 28 10 Common mistakes beginner investors make and how to avoid them

Number 1

The mistake: Confusing a nominal yield with a real yield. To think that it is easy to have a return above the average and that it is mediocre to invest in order to aim at the average market yield.

What you need to know: The average return is provided by economic growth. To have an excess return it is necessary that someone else in the market has a sub-reward.

A good answer to the error: Invest in index funds or ETF funds to have healthy long-term returns. Add liquidity or bonds to adjust the risk / return ratio.

Number 2

The mistake: Buy only shares of well-managed companies

What you need to know: The stock is not the company! The difference lies in the price you pay for the share.

A good answer to the error: Buy investment instruments that diversify widely, such as ETFs or index funds

Number 3

The mistake: To think that if a financial instrument has given good returns in the past it is more likely that it will continue to do so in the future. Pay management fees based on past returns.

What you need to know: The financial markets are completely unpredictable. Every prediction on them has a probability of realizing (or not to be realized) oscillating between 40 and 60%

A good answer to the error: Do not pay commissions for active management based on past returns. Investing in the main categories of investments (stocks, bonds, real estate, liquid assets and alternative instruments) based on your financial objectives, tolerance and propensity for financial risk.

Number 4

The mistake: Making decisions on individual financial instruments and not from the perspective of the portfolio as a whole.

What you need to know: The risk characteristics of the portfolio complex are largely predictable.

A good answer to the error: Pay attention to a good diversification of the portfolio complex that combines with the right dose of risk based on your objectives and possibilities.

Number 5

The mistake: To think that commissions, technical costs and taxation are not important.

What you need to know: The management of savings in America costs an average of 3% per year. In the long run, this cost has a dramatic impact on the actual compound return.

A good answer to the error: Use simple securities for the bond component of the portfolio, ETF or funds indexed to low management fees for the equity part.

Number 6

The mistake: Having all the savings in bank accounts or monetary instruments.

What you need to know: Financial markets pay a non-diversifiable "risk premium"

A good answer to the error: Having a well-diversified portfolio allows you to have additional income to the one deriving from your job.

Number 7

The mistake: To panic when things go wrong and be greedy when things go well

What you need to know: Future performance expectations have very little relationship to past returns.

A good answer to the error: Base the composition of the financial portfolio on the long-term expected risk / return ratio.

Number 8

The mistake: Never make changes to the composition of the portfolio even when your assets, due to markets or personal situations, have changed.

What you need to know: Some market fluctuations can generate non-recoverable losses with a normal financial market trend. The right ratio between risk / return is strongly influenced also by the consistency of the assets.

A good answer to the error: Check carefully what is the maximum bearable loss (in absolute value) on the basis of its assets, and make the relevant adjustments in the investment components to comply with this risk constraint.

Number 9

The mistake: Spend a lot of time with newspapers, TV and financial websites.

What you need to know: The non-diversifiable risk, the decrease in costs and taxes maintain their value even when they are used by everyone, the ideas for having extra-financial returns.

A good answer to the error: Do not try to buy the "right" stock or enter and exit at the "right time". Only liars can do it.

Number 10

The mistake: Relying on consultants who are good at moving the portfolio on the basis of unlikely forecasts of future market movements or paying high commissions for unproductive management of mutual funds or asset management.

What you need to know: The vast majority of financial services are structured in such a way as to produce powerful conflicts of interest between the client and the intermediaries. Since the client is the weaker party because it has less knowledge, these conflicts of interest translate into completely unproductive costs.

A good answer to the error: Consider the possibility of relying on independent financial planners paid only to parcels and money managers who keep commission levels very low and emphasize financial risk management rather than returns.

Conclusion

Well, you have made it to the end of the book

Becoming a self-directed investor is an exciting way to take charge of your finances. It is great to take ownership and begin to control your own financial future. This can help you in many ways, not the least of which is getting to a position of financial independence. Unfortunately, most people never get there. But now that you've begun educating yourself, you have also begun to acquire the knowledge and tools you need to achieve it yourself.

Take your time in carefully considering what times of the day you will allocate to trading and set yourself up with an environment that allows you the most opportunity to focus and make level headed decisions. Remember your emotions and keep them in check. We should never underestimate how our feelings and emotions come into play when it comes to trading. Prepare yourself for the fact that there will be losses, and you will win some and lose some. Above all, stay calm and learn from any mistakes you may make.

Just remember to say in the markets for the long-term. That is the first rule of success. Traders are trying to sell people on the promise of quick cash, but long-term investing remains the best way to build wealth for the future.

You should build a highly diversified portfolio. It can include some individual stocks, but it should also include exchange-traded funds. They should be diverse as well, so you should have funds in your account that track major stock market indices, but also funds that track sectors, real estate, and energy. Also, be sure to do some bond investing through your exchange-traded funds. A diversified portfolio is a winning portfolio — every time.

Finally, make sure to follow the principles of dollar cost averaging. This not only helps you with averaging out your costs so that you're not mistakenly buying stocks always at price peaks. Dollar cost averaging also keeps you in the habit of investing regularly. Many people fail to keep up, and then years later, they find their investments are not as large as they had hoped. By following a program of regularly investing, you can ensure that you get to a place where you want to go.

Thanks again for reaching the end of this book! Let's hope it has been informative and able to provide you with all of the tools you need to achieve your goals whatever they may be.

The next step is to:

- Get Started and Pursue Your Dreams: Passion fuels focus, resilience, and perseverance. You need to have all three of these characteristics of a successful forex trader in order to pursue your dreams and your goals.

- **Practice Makes Perfect:** Research has shown that the human brain is functioning at its highest when it has had at least an hour and a half in one activity or another. That's why you see athletes and people who play musical instruments practice rigorously, every single day, and still maintain their rest. Relative to you as a new trader, this tells you that you need to allow yourself time to do other things. While this is a business, you don't want it to consume your life. Master the larger charts first. This also allows you to come back refreshed when we come back to it. The market is not going anywhere—trust me.

- **Ask for Feedback, It's Okay:** You want someone who can break it down for you without being pompous and scholarly. That won't help you to make the necessary changes to your strategy. The most successful traders have identified what is working for them but are also constantly seeking the feedback of experts.

- **Document:** You will realize the significance of having all of your progress in an organized journal as you gain more experience. You will essentially have a visual for your risk management and profit strategies right there for you. This helps you keep the mindset needed and we have talked about for trading. This is the quickest way to success, by far.

- Get your demo account, and start trading. Don't be scared. You have everything you need to get started. It's go time! I know that once you put these strategies and practices in place, you will be on your way to earning a profit in no time!